TITANIA'S BOOK OF HOURS

A CELEBRATION OF THE WITCH'S YEAR

TITANIA'S BOOK OF HOURS

A CELEBRATION OF THE WITCH'S YEAR

TITANIA HARDIE

PHOTOGRAPHS BY SARA MORRIS

QUADRILLE PUBLISHING

For Anne Furniss, who has always believed in me, and Sara Morris, who has an enchanted eye. Thanks both.

'TRUTH IS THE DAUGHTER OF TIME'
Old Proverb

Also by Titania Hardie
HOCUS POCUS: Titania's Book of Spells
BEWITCHED: Titania's Book of Love Spells
TITANIA'S ORAQLE: A Unique Way to Predict Your Future
TITANIA'S WISHING SPELLS: Health, Wealth, Love, Happiness, Peace, Harmony
ENCHANTED: Titania's Book of White Magic
ZILLIONZ: Titania's Book of Numerology
TITANIA'S FORTUNE CARDS
WHITE MAGIC: Titania's Complete Book of Spells
TITANIA'S SPELL CARDS: Love & Success, Health & Happiness, Peace & Harmony
HUBBLE BUBBLE: Titania's Book of Magical Feasts
LOVE POTIONS: Titania's Book of Romantic Elixirs

First published in 2002 by Quadrille Publishing Limited
Alhambra House, 27-31 Charing Cross Road,
London WC2H OLS

PUBLISHER Anne Furniss
DESIGN Jim Smith
EDITORIAL ASSISTANT Katie Ginn
PRODUCTION Tracy Hart, Vincent Smith

BRITISH LIBRARY CATALOGUING IN PUBLICATION DATA
A catalogue record for this book is available from the British Library
ISBN 1 903845 84 X

Printed and bound in Germany

The publishers would like to acknowledge thanks for permission
to use the Greenman wall plaque by David Lawrence (page 52)
www.fromthegreenwood.com

XII
I
II
III
IV
V
VI
VII
VIII
IX
X
XI

Introducing the magical cycle of life : OUR ANCESTORS

SAW THE CALENDAR OF OUR DAYS AND HOURS AS MARKING POINTS ON A GREAT WHEEL OF LIFE. The perpetuation of our species was dependent upon a close relationship with the natural cycles of time: marking the seasons, understanding the pull of the moon, celebrating the power of the sun. These cycles were seen, poetically, as phases in harmony with the birth, the life, the death, and the rebirth of the goddess, primarily, and of the god too. For a harmonious existence, it was important to shadow these moments – 'as above, so below'. ❧ WITCHES WORK CLOSELY WITH THE 'OLD WAY' OF LOOKING AT THINGS, BECAUSE IT RECOGNISES THE NATURAL RHYTHMS OF THE EARTH, AND THE NATURAL HIGH AND LOW POINTS OF THE SEASONS AND THE PLANETS. Rather than seeing the earth simply as gas and rock and water, it is an invitation to see it still as a mother-nurturer – our home. To keep the world turning happily, and to encourage the return of the waning sun and the correct behaviour at the dying year, the force of 'earth magic' was employed. This was to caress the little mid-points – like spokes in the wheel of the year – into their next forward movement. ❧ THOSE MIDPOINTS ARE THE SOLAR AND THE LUNAR FESTIVALS – OR SABBATS. The Winter Solstice is the shortest day of the year, measuring the happy moment from which the sun will grow stronger again. This is December 21st in the northern hemisphere (Yule), and June 21st in the southern. At the Spring Equinox, day and night are of equal length – just as they are at the Autumn Equinox. In the north, the Spring Equinox is March 21st and the Autumn Equinox is September 21st, whereas in the southern hemisphere, again, those dates are reversed. The Summer Solstice, of course, is the longest day – June 21st for dwellers in the north, and December 21st for Antipodeans. ❧ THE LUNAR FESTIVALS RETAIN THEIR CELTIC NAMES, AND THESE MARK THE MOON'S MOST IMPORTANT CYCLES. Samhain, also called Hallowe'en, is the start of winter, the Celtic New Year, and it equates to the so-called 'dark moon'. This is October 31st. Beltane is its opposite, also called 'May Day', and celebrates the arrival of summer – the full moon. This is May 1st. Imbolc is the first day of spring – very early spring – and equates to the waxing (or growing) moon. This is February 1st. Its co-ordinate point is August 1st, the festival of Lughnasadh (pronounced 'loonassa'), which initiates the start of the autumnal moon, or the waning moon. In the southern hemisphere, these dates are also reversed. The Christian names of Lammas (for Lughnasadh) and Candlemas (for Imbolc) may be more familiar.

The book of hours :

A Book of Hours was, from medieval times, a prized possession, inscribing the religious devotions that belonged to the (Catholic) year. Hand-painted and bound, they were expensive, belonging to the aristocracy, and often individually commissioned. ❧ The purpose of our Book of Hours is to help you unlock the meaning and purpose of pagan and pre-Christian celebratory days, and indeed the entire calendar year, as they have affected the ideas behind Wicca and witchcraft. This way you can connect the significance of your magic with its ideological origins, and work it most easily in accordance with its design. Celebrating and recognising the earth's cycle through the year is a rich tradition handed down from our ancestors, which has been evolving since the dawn of time. Whilst I would be the first to agree that much 'magical' practice does indeed stem from superstitious ideas and fears, I personally feel that magic is an expression of our inner psyche. This could be described as a sense of wonder at the light of the moon and the sun, an awareness of their individual impacts on our own behaviour, and an acknowledgement of the importance of seasons and cycles. Working with that knowledge we can survive seasonal, climatic and personal difficulties by adopting a particular frame of mind. ❧ As we now scientifically recognise the existence of S.A.D. (Seasonal Adjustment Disorder), we can comprehend the attention paid to the seasons, and the celebratory rituals designed to mark the darkest and coldest – or longest and hottest – days, that our ancestors felt compelled to enact. We understand what they were experiencing. Indeed, I believe that much of the ritual of the past acted as a form of communal treatment for what we might now call the tensions and stresses of life. And so, too, magical forces are most potent when the rivers run highest, or the sun beats strongest, or the storms strike hardest. Some spell-making and mind-focus works on a high solar energy, some on lower, and likewise with the moons. ❧ There are traditional spells and tasks associated with the unfolding of the year, so that you can work magic on a regular basis throughout the year. We will look at the significance of each day of the week, and of each moon; we will celebrate the seasons with appropriate activity and spell-making, and we will work rituals at each proper sabbat. This is easy to do, and only takes a short time to become a part of one's life. ❧ Finally, we will look at our own individual calendars – observing magical ways by which we can recognise and enshrine those dates that mean something to us individually. These will include blessing a new home and even choosing the best day to move; celebrating an engagement or anniversary; or finding a 'witchy' and magical way to mark the birth of a child, or their name day. ❧ Together we can

QUIETLY INJECT MAGIC INTO ALL THE DAYS OF OUR LIVES, SURVIVING LOW TIDES AND RIDING TRIUMPHANT ON HIGH ONES. We will carry our own inner sunshine through wintry chill, and keep cool and relaxed with magical awareness through the sun's zenith at high summer. We will dream brightly under a Beltane moon, and send mysterious thoughts on a watery, waning one. We will live close to the earth's pulse, and borrow from its resistance. En route, perhaps, we will have learned how to live in greater harmony with the earth and our neighbours, and we will understand how to admire her amazing treasures, and use them more wisely. ❧ RAINBOWS OF BLESSINGS.

A ritual consecration to the elements ❧ HERE IS A RITUAL

FOR THE DAY ON WHICH YOU DECIDE TO START PRACTISING MAGIC. It is simple, but it will enhance your spell-making powers if you perform this rite. ❧ CHOOSE A WOODEN-HANDLED KNIFE, WITH WHICH YOU WILL CUT HERBS AND BOUGHS OF FLOWERS FOR MAGICAL PURPOSES. Wrap it in a soft cloth and produce it on a full moon if possible. Go to a private and natural space – it may be your garden or balcony if you live in a city, but traditionally it would be at the epicentre of magical forces. This translates as a place preferably near running water, near a hill, near some woods or at least several trees, but you could adapt this to your environment. ❧ PLUNGE THE KNIFE INTO THE EARTH, HANDLE POINTING SKYWARDS, AND KNEEL, FIRST FACING NORTH, SAYING: *"I conjure thee, blade of steel, by the powers of the earth, to aid me in the art of my magical practice, performed for good and not for ill"*. After about a minute, grasp the handle and remove the knife from the ground, pointing it to the heavens. Then continue by climbing the hill, or an incline or slope. Now face towards the east, and say: *"I conjure thee, blade of steel, by the powers of the wind, to serve me in my arts of magical practice, for good and not for ill"*. You should then light a small fire – or use a large candle – and face south, saying: *"I conjure thee, blade of steel, by the power of fire, to aid me in my magical arts, for good and never for ill"*, then pass the blade through the flame. Finally, facing west, dip the knife into the water, and say: *"I conjure thee, blade of steel, by the power of the waters, to aid me in my magical craft, always for good and never for ill"*. ❧ THE KNIFE SHOULD NOW BE PLACED ONCE AGAIN IN THE CLEAN SOFT CLOTH, THE FLAMES DOUSED WITH SOME OF THE WATER, AND YOUR ARMS SHOULD FORM AN ARC IN EACH DIRECTION AS YOU LEAVE THE SPOT – first north, then east, then south, and finally west. Bow, and say, *"Blessed be"*. ❧ YOUR INSTRUMENT IS NOW READY FOR ALL YOUR MAGICAL WORK, AND YOU SHOULD TRY ALWAYS TO CUT YOUR HERBS AND FLOWERS WITH THIS MAGICAL TOOL.

THE WITCH'S
WEEK

Of

COURSE, EVERYONE KNOWS
THAT MIDNIGHT IS THE 'WITCHING HOUR' –
THE BEST TIME TO PERFORM MAGIC, BECAUSE THE
EARTH SLEEPS, YOUR MENTAL POWERS ARE AT THEIR MOST
INTENSE, AND YOU ARE LEAST LIKELY TO BE DISTURBED. BUT
CERTAIN DAYS OF THE WEEK ARE ALSO MORE PROPITIOUS
FOR PARTICULAR MAGICAL CEREMONIES. IN EVERY LANGUAGE,
THE NAMES OF THE DAYS OF THE WEEK CAN STILL BE TRACED BACK
TO THE PAGAN DEITIES WHOSE POWERS WERE SYNONYMOUS WITH
THE ENERGY OF EACH INDIVIDUAL DAY. IF YOU WORK WITH THIS
ANCIENT SPIRIT, AND HARMONISE WITH THE FORCES THAT WERE SAID
TO BE AT THEIR PEAK ON ANY ONE DAY, YOU MAY BE SURPRISED AT
THE STRENGTH OF YOUR THOUGHT. MAGIC CAN BE DESCRIBED
AS CHANGE WROUGHT THROUGH THE POWER OF THOUGHT
AND THE PSYCHE, AND MAGIC WORKED ON ITS 'TRUE'
DAY OF THE WEEK WILL UTILISE THE HIDDEN
STORE OF THAT PSYCHE WITH
GREATER POETRY.

Monday: the moon's day : You need never dread that 'Monday morning feeling' again if you approach the start of the working week with the right attitude. Honour the day, and it will treat you gently. : Monday is dedicated to the moon, and I have begun the week on this day (rather than Sunday) to commence with the power of female energy rather than the male energy of the sun. : Any magic you work on a Monday should incorporate the use of a moonstone and/or silver, and any spell you cast should properly concern the subjects of woman/motherhood (but leave matters of love for Friday), the family, hearth and home, dreams and visions, or the sea. : On any Monday, whether you have magic to perform or not, start by honouring the day. Light a silvery, moonlight-coloured candle, or one which favours the sea (blue-green or turquoise), and make a short wish for female strength and insight, and for kindness from the world around you. Do this for a few minutes before you leave the house in the morning.

A Monday spell for good luck : Gather together a candle as before, a pearl or moonstone, something silver, a white ribbon and a white flower – usually a rose or a poppy, although a little sprig of watercress (sacred to the moon) would do nicely. If you want even more power in your magic, honour the moon's rule over the sea and add a shell, a seahorse, a dish of salt, or any other seaside connection you have, such as a boat, pebbles or driftwood. : Work early in the morning or late at night, perhaps in the comfort of your bedroom. Place your items around the candle and light it; close your eyes and envisage your desired goal. Speak some words of feminine entreaty to Diana, goddess of the moon, then smile or laugh and extinguish the flame. If you have held the thought clearly in your heart and head for a few moments, luck and power will be reflected in your life.

Magical tip: For general good feeling on a Monday, always wear silver or pearls. Remember that a white rose is sacred to the day, so put one in a little glass near you to attract power and positivity.

Tuesday: the day of Mars, god of war : NEVER AS

EXCITING AS THURSDAY OR FRIDAY, NOR AS DIFFICULT TO RISE FROM BED FOR AS MONDAY, TUESDAY IS OFTEN FELT TO BE UNIMPORTANT. Magically, however, this is the day for going into action, resolving (or initiating) matters of conflict and dealing with matters of sexuality. Tuesday also rules hunting, masculinity, physical strength and courage, lust and issues concerned with fieriness. Honeysuckle and opals are sacred to the rites of Tuesday, especially if the opal is flecked with 'fire', but a cornelian (bloodstone), a red ruby or a garnet can also be used. **:** TUESDAY IS AN APPROPRIATE DAY FOR WORKING A LOVE SPELL IF A LACK OF PHYSICAL CONSUMMATION HAS BEEN THE PROBLEM. First, make up a blend of scented oils: add a few drops of black pepper and jasmine or vanilla essential oils to 25 ml alcohol and leave for 48 hours. On a Tuesday evening, light a red candle girdled with a red ribbon with your lover's name 'sealed' to it with sealing wax. Surround yourself in red light and imagine it penetrating your erogenous zones. Spray a little peppery scent on your chest near your heart. You will now ooze with extraordinary sensual charm and confidence. You could also massage a little jasmine oil into your ankles to spark your wild side.

A plea for strength : PERHAPS YOU ARE A GENTLE SOUL, STEELING YOURSELF TO SAY

SOMETHING IMPORTANT BUT DIFFICULT TO SOMEONE, AND YOU FEEL IT MAY REQUIRE MORE AGGRESSION THAN YOU NORMALLY HAVE. At such a moment, you can invoke the gods of war to lend you the strength for a combat – even if it is a gentle-hearted one. **:** ON A TUESDAY MORNING, GATHER TOGETHER A RED FLOWER, SOME HONEYSUCKLE OR A FRESH RADISH OR SOME MUSTARD CRESS, AS WELL AS A RED STONE OR OPAL AND SOMETHING MADE FROM IRON OR STEEL (THIS LAST TO SYMBOLISE YOUR DETERMINATION TO BE FLINTIER THAN USUAL). Place them in front of a red candle and light it. As you do so, address Mars (think of him as the handsome hunk seduced by Venus in the Botticelli painting if you find a pure war god untenable) and ask him for the strength to tackle somebody about an issue that concerns you. Close your eyes and see yourself powerfully addressing your 'foe' and having 'the last word' – which stands for the final enchantment. Blow out your candle and utter a quick thanks. **:** YOU MUST CONTRIVE TO HAVE THE WORDS OUT AND SAID WITHIN A VERY SHORT TIME, PREFERABLY THAT VERY DAY. If you have properly imagined yourself girded for 'war', you will soon find that you take gentle command of the situation and achieve the result you desire.

Wednesday: the day of Woden : I HAVE ALWAYS FOUND CHILDREN

BORN ON A WEDNESDAY TO BE ESPECIALLY LUCKY IN THEIR POWERS OF SPEECH AND PERSUASION. The day is traditionally sacred to the all-powerful Woden (or Odin), the father god and magician, charmer with words, who is also related to the Roman god Mercury and the Greek Hermes, both also magical messengers and magicians. ❧ WEDNESDAY RULES BOTH CONSCIOUS AND UNCONSCIOUS MENTAL PROWESS: STUDY, SPOKEN MESSAGES, LETTERS AND COMMUNICATIONS OF ALL KINDS, TELEPATHY, DIVINATION AND PREDICTIONS. Sacred to Wednesday are the hazel tree, mulberry and lily-of-the-valley, the gems sapphire and amethyst, the metal mercury (quicksilver) and the colour violet. ❧ FOR LUCK IN YOUR STUDIES, OR WITH ANYTHING CONCERNING THE GIVING OF A SPEECH OR A TALK, DO THE FOLLOWING ON A WEDNESDAY MORNING. Honour the deity in your own simple words, place one of the above flowers or a hazelnut beside a very small violet-coloured candle and ask for extra power and sway in the day ahead. Light the candle and make a very quick wish, seeing the task before you melt into pleasure and achieving pure joy. Blow out the flame and wave your hand once through the smoke. Success is yours for the taking!

Sending a message by magical means : NO NEED TO GO

TO THE BOTHER OF POSTING LETTERS WHEN YOU CAN COMMUNICATE IN THIS WAY. On a Wednesday after 7.00 p.m., send a mental message to a friend you want to contact, or imagine saying simple words you find difficult to phrase face-to-face, perhaps to heal a quarrel or express emotion. ❧ PUT A PHOTO OF THE RECIPIENT IN FRONT OF YOU AND INVOKE WODEN, OR MERCURY, OR HERMES. Light a violet-coloured candle, and use a hazelnut or rod to forge contact between you and the gods and the person you would speak with. Roll the hazelnut or rod in your hand and wave this same hand or wand over the picture. Speak the words you wish to say very gently; you might simply articulate: *"Please get in touch"*, or *"I'm sorry we quarrelled"*, or *"Could you express your feelings for me a little more"*, or something of this nature. Blow out the candle only after you have phrased some words of thanks to the deity of Wednesday. Leave the hazelnut near the photo of your friend. You will shortly find your thoughts have been communicated to the one you wish to contact.

Magical tip: On a Wednesday, place your own photo next to a hazelnut or rod on a high shelf from dawn till dusk for an unusually witty, communicative and lucky day. Also, send even the briefest note to someone on a Wednesday to spread magic.

Thursday: the day of Thor

A VERY LUCKY DAY, BELONGING TO THE ROMAN JUPITER, THE GREEK ZEUS AND THE NORSE AND TEUTONIC EQUIVALENT THOR ('THE THUNDERER'). Dedicate this day to issues concerning luck and prosperity, legal matters, high honours and all forms of material expansion. Thor, Zeus and Jupiter are all connected with the oak and thus with mistletoe, most prized by the Druids. This was the day thought to have the greatest power and connection with the strongest gods until supplanted by Sunday, when the Emperor Constantine pronounced it as the day of the Lord. However, Thursday is still regarded as the most potent day for witchcraft – and it is the child born on this day who is said to have 'far to go'. SACRED TO THURSDAY IS ANYTHING CONNECTED WITH OAK LEAVES AND TREES, ACORNS, OR MISTLETOE; also storms and heavy rain – so a storm on a Thursday is sent by the gods and should be revelled in, or danced in – Gene Kelly style! Powerfully scented red carnations and borage (aptly called 'starflower'), are also sacred to Thursday, as well as the metal tin – though when addressing the gods, it should be done with white gold (on Sunday use yellow gold). Opinion is divided as to whether the gemstone should be diamond or topaz, but I prefer the more precious stone because of the ancient tradition of this day being one of prosperity and financial power.

To attract success and prosperity

THURSDAY, THEN, IS THE KEY DAY FOR MATERIAL MATTERS. If you need a new job, or want promotion, light a green or gold candle every Thursday for a month, starting with a waning moon to magnetise bad luck away, then on the waxing moon to attract a new and positive contract or opportunity to you. Have a purification bath filled with oak leaves, do anything with an oak leaf or tree that honours it, and burn woody incense. Cut a golden bough of mistletoe to invoke the wisdom of the gods to help you in a new life, and even after Christmas, retain a few leaves or berries somewhere precious, which was traditionally in a white cloth. If you really want divine intervention, you should cut some mistletoe with a golden blade – though admittedly, this could be tricky. Keep a little gold chain with the sprig instead, for gold is sacred to the gods, whereas iron keeps supernatural energy at bay. Most importantly, sleep on a diamond – the tiniest one will do – and wear a little diamond until your luck waxes. Always honour the day and look for that huge planet Jupiter in the night sky.

Magical tip: Walk out in a storm on a Thursday, turn your face to the skies, thank the heavens for all you have and wish for providence continuing.

Friday: sacred to Freya Freya is the Norse love goddess, a creature of charm and sensuous fertility, also called Frigg, whose equivalent is Venus or Aphrodite; the name of Venus finds echoes in the French and Italian names for Friday – Vendredi and Venerdi. This is the perfect day for a love spell, but also for other Venusian attributes – spells and rituals for pleasure, perfume-making and buying, issues concerned with beauty and eroticism, with music and the arts. Sacred to Friday is the rose, personal emblem of the love goddess. Pink or red are traditional love roses, whereas white is chaste and suits the moon. Extra special potency comes on a Friday from a wild rose. On a Friday, make a simple shrine to honour the love goddess – place a single stem or odd number of roses in a vase, and drop in a small crystal or semi-precious stone. Do this if you would bring added joys, brighter pleasures, a more artistic spark, or of course, luck in love, on a Friday The sacred gemstone of Venus and Friday is the beautiful emerald, symbolic of love and success, or alternatively tourmaline, symbolic of hope. Worn on a Friday, either will bestow luck and lend you flashes of imagination and sensuality.

An easy love spell for a Friday This can be performed in five minutes at either end of the day, around 6.00–7.00 a.m. or p.m. Light a pink or rose-scented candle, address your goddess, ask for her friendship and blessings today and express to her in a few simple words any worry or doubt or problem you are experiencing in the area of love or emotional partnerships. Ask her to find you a space in the day to help you clear up this difficulty with your loved one, ending with the words: *"So mote it be"*. Blow out the candle very fast, like a wish on a birthday cake, then see if you can spot Venus in the morning or evening sky, a very twinkly blue star. Now set out for the day or evening ahead feeling warmly humorous and very confident.

Magical tips: Make a special love charm – a piece of jewellery, key ring or other accessory – on a Friday. Plant any seedling dedicated to finding a brand new love on this day. Make this the evening on which you invite someone you love into your home, or out for dinner. Roses must be worn in some form, and the scent of them should fill the air, honouring Venus. Be sure, too, to eat an apple, wishing as you cut across it to reveal the 'star' in the centre.

Saturday: Saturn's day :

FOR MOST OF US, SATURDAY IS THE START OF THE WEEKEND, YET SATURN IS THE TASK-MASTER OF THE GODS, WHOSE CONCERNS ARE HARD WORK, COMMON SENSE, PROVIDING SENSIBLY AND SECURING PROPERTY. So perhaps it makes some sense that we now spend so much time doing our household chores on Saturdays : THIS IS CERTAINLY THE DAY FOR PROPERTY TRANSACTIONS AND MAGICALLY IS AN IDEAL DAY TO MOVE HOUSE. Spells to find houses or protect your home should be performed on this day. Rowan trees are often used in property magic, so a rowan twig bound to a house key and a dark green or earth brown candle, lit and dedicated to Saturn will ensure security in your home. : THE SNOWDROP EMPATHISES WITH SATURDAY. SATURN WAS THE LORD OF DEATH AND RULER OF THE NIGHT, INCLUDING THE DARK OF MIDWINTER. The snowdrop is the first consolation that Saturn brings back something from what was taken. Always view snowdrops with a sense of replenishment, a reminder that we can recover from waning times in our affairs through hard work and dedication. Hellebores (Christmas roses), comfrey and ivy are also sacred to Saturn.

A ritual for moving into a new home :

IF POSSIBLE, CHOOSE A WAXING MOON FOR THE MOVE, FOR YOU ARE GROWING INTO SOMETHING POSITIVE. : HAVE ONE OF YOUR NEW DOOR KEYS SILVER-PLATED BY A KEY-CUTTER (OR YOU COULD SPRAY IT SILVER OR COVER IT IN SILVER FOIL). Show the key to the moon the night before you turn it in the lock and ask for blessings and happy dreams inside your dwelling. On the day you move in, place a strand of pink, green or white ribbon across the threshold and tie a fragment of it around the top of the key, too. Use a pair of scissors to cut through the ribbon with your loved one/s, and make a wish. Take the silver key and place it inside a shell near a candle or fireplace, and burn some incense just near it – pine or benzoin (or orange if you're newly married) – to cast out negative thoughts and usher in strong new ones. Light the fire or candle, and see a happy home and hearth enveloping you. Ask for protection, especially from fire. Restore the key (with the ribbon) to a lucky place, and use it only symbolically. : YOUR HOUSE MOVE WOULD BE COMPLETELY BLESSED IF YOU COULD PLANT A ROWAN TREE OR A WILLOW IN THE GARDEN OR IN A LARGE POT, ASKING THAT THE GODS SMILE ON YOUR SPACE.

Magical tip: Put a sundial in your garden or on a patio, if you have room, to honour Saturn who also rules time. Make sure snowdrops are planted near it and perhaps also hellebores and ivy.

Sunday: day of the bright sun : ORIGINALLY SACRED TO APOLLO AND
THE SUN AND THEREAFTER TO GOD, THIS IS THE DAY OF MAXIMUM POWER, AND SHOULD BE COMMEMORATED WITH FIRE.
: SUNDAY IS THE DAY FOR GENERAL SPELLS, FOR IDEAS CONCERNING PEOPLE IN CHARGE, SUCH AS WORLD LEADERS AND POLITICIANS, OR EMPLOYERS ON THE GRAND SCALE. It is also connected with health and healing, friendship in the broadest sense, but also with holidays and fun. Work some magic on a Sunday if you need time off or want to plan a feast such as a wedding or party. This will ensure your celebration goes like a rocket. This is also the day to think thoughts and make wishes which concern men around you in positions of power or authority. : SUNDAY IS THE BEST DAY TO HONOUR THE SUNSHINE HOURS, ESPECIALLY IN THE GARDEN, AND TO MAKE TIME FOR PERSONAL PEACE AND REST. We must remember this, for increasingly our leisure hours are swallowed up with work of some kind. Even if you must work on a Sunday, make one hour for rest, peace and to honour the sun – the more so if the day itself is grey. : SUNDAY'S COLOURS ARE SUNSHINE YELLOW, ORANGE, YELLOW GOLD AND EVEN THE COLOURS OF THE RAINBOW. Its gem is the potent ruby and sometimes the peridot. The flowers are many, all flowers of joy and healing. They include sunflowers and marigolds, but also the spice saffron, the yellow-hued heartsease (pansy) and the celandine. More recently, citrus flowers (such as orange blossom and bergamot) and even the tiger lily have been connected with the sun and Sunday. : IF YOU WOULD LIKE TO EMIT AN AURA OF RADIANT CONFIDENCE AND HAPPINESS, CHOOSE A SUNDAY TO WORK THIS RITUAL. Choose a candle from the sunshine colour spectrum, a citrus scent and a tall, yellow flower and bring them together early on a Sunday. Toast the sun with citrus juice and make a vow both to honour the spirit of rest and the spirit of solar power in some way today. Tie a yellow ribbon around your wrist to harness the energy from your short ritual.

A magical ritual of thanks and blessing : WHENEVER
YOU WANT TO SAY A HUGE COSMIC 'THANK YOU', THIS IS THE DAY – IN OR OUT OF DOORS. To honour friends and friendship and particularly peace among men, light a fire, a barbecue, or a candle, and send your thoughts of thanks and blessings into the ether. Scent the atmosphere with orange and clove, and wink or blow a kiss to the sun itself, even when it is obscured by cloud. Merit will attend you and if it has been raining a rainbow may well appear. **Magical tip: Close your eyes and turn your lashes to the brightest sunlight. Make a short unselfish wish and smile. Your Sunday will blossom.**

MOON
CYCLES

XII   I   II   III   IIII   V   VI   VII   VIII   IX   X   XI

In Italian witchcraft, Aradia is queen of the witches, bestower of wisdom and secrets. Daughter of Diana, the moon, and the sun, Aradia imparts celestial knowledge to those with a wise mind and a courageous heart. The owl and the hare are her night-messengers. Witches recognise the importance of flowing with nature's rhythms, seeing in our own nature the reflection of the moon's orbit around the sun (roughly 28 days with a strong connotation for women), and the earth's rotation across one year. Knowing that the moon rules the tides and being ourselves made up of a high content of water, we can maximise the energy of our lives by understanding this lunar influence. As the moon waxes from darkness to brightness, then wanes to darkness again, the cycle of human life — birth, adolescence, adulthood, death, then rebirth — are reflected and understood.

New moon : THE WAXING, GROWING MOON BRINGS MOISTURE, THE RISING TIDE AND THE FLOW

OF ALL LIFE. This is especially so with plant life and the first 14 days of the moon's cycle offer the best time for sowing seeds, giving baby plants the opportunity to swell and ripen with the waxing moon. Similarly, we as individuals feel a quickening impulse with the growing moon. **❧** SOMETIMES THE BRAND NEW MOON, WHICH LASTS ONLY FOR A DAY, IS INVISIBLE AS IT IS OBSCURED BY THE LIGHT OF THE SUN, MAKING JUST A VAGUE, SHADOWY OUTLINE. Women often feel more vulnerable at this time and may respond emotionally. **❧** UNDER THE DREAMY SPELL OF THE 'MAIDEN MOON', DIANA IN HER FIRST BLUSH OF MAIDENHOOD IS THE CLEAREST EXAMPLE OF GROWING POTENTIAL AND PURITY. Now is the moment to enact a spell dedicated to a new beginning in any realm: love, work or home. This most open moment of personal consciousness is a good time to meditate without particular questions in mind, as you will be at your most receptive. Be ready for inspirational thought. **❧** FOR A 'NEW MOON' SPELL YOU NEED GOSSAMER-THIN THREADS, THE SILVER HOAR FROSTS OR SILKY SNAIL TRAILS OF NATURE. If you find a great silvery web, stand before it to speak your intent towards a new project or person in your life. Dress in white like invisible silvery light. Talk to the east, where sun and moon both rise. Even better, if a snail has left a trail across your path, or the frost has kissed the grass around you with silvery breath, and you come upon either of these things under the new moon, stop and address Diana and her daughter, Aradia. Ask for feminine inspiration, crystal clear vision and understanding, and the blossoming of new thoughts. Ask for help in launching one important new project, and the goddess will hear you.

Crescent moon : THIS IS THE FIRST OBVIOUS APPEARANCE OF THE WAXING MOON, AS IT

BEGINS TO SWELL IN ITS OUTLINE BEYOND THE NEW MOON TOWARDS THE FIRST QUARTER. Look for this pretty moon in the afternoon sky towards the setting sun, lasting for several days. **❧** THIS IS THE MOON OF CONTINUING DEDICATION, TREATED MAGICALLY LIKE THE NEW MOON. The waxing energy is conducive to growing thought and inspiration, and personal energy is also waxing. For the first 14 days of the moon cycle we are at peak energy to begin new projects and carry them through. **❧** CONTINUE RITUAL FOR A NEW OPENING – PERHAPS WORKING A SPELL THAT UNFOLDS OVER SEVEN DAYS – AND INCORPORATE YOUNG PLANT SEEDLINGS. Place a sprig of foliage in a silver ring by a white candle, with an invocation stating your desire for new things. Tend it for seven days, as near as possible to the appearance, late in the afternoon, of the crescent moon in the sky. Anything you ask for in a tone of unselfish, maiden innocence will be granted as the moon continues to wax.

Waxing half moon :

The first quarter, or half moon, occurs about one week after the moon was new. Now you can see the moon from the middle of the day to about midnight, connecting it with the field of dreams. You should conceptualise the growing tangibility of your magic-making and wishes; you might try to surround anything very important to you with a beautiful, bright silver light in your mind's eye so you may learn something intuitive to help you in that area. Actual messages may suddenly materialise that point you in a very important direction. ❧ Progress from verbal magic, where you speak out your wishes (called invocation) to thought – practise holding one idea in your mind for several minutes without chatter. While looking at the moon for a few minutes, visualise the appearance of amazing things in your life: achievements, social harmony, success in work, growing love relationships, possibly fertility, or finding a happy home. See your plans forming into actualities against the half-circle now brightly visible in the sky. Whisper words, rather than speaking them loudly, and be gentle and soft-spoken with your friends.

Gibbous moon :

The last slip-thread before the moon is truly full, this beautiful moon rises near sunset and is full of promise. This is the last moment before peak fertility at full moon. Close your eyes and let your mind drift back to a moment that made you truly happy. If this makes you smile, wish upon the moon and your full, fecund power of imagination to open up many new moments of future true happiness. ❧ Your emotions are at full tilt now, so this is a perfect time for casting deep love spells, or magic connected with relationships or fertility. Open your eyes to the light of the moon, and say: *"Diana (or Tana, or indeed another variant is Titania, or Selene), spirit of the moon, With your deep understanding of the souls of men and women, Beautiful Diana, by the reverence I give thee, And the joy of love which you have ever seen and known, Guardian of our secret thought and night-time hopes: Grant me aid in my love, and my heart's fond desire, which I do swear will cause harm unto none. So mote it be."* (It is perfectly acceptable to read this out from the book, under the light of the moon with a candle, rather than trying to memorise it). Now place a silver talisman of a dog, an owl, or a hare – the messengers of the moon – up to the moon's glow. See the moon's face transform into the face of your loved one and express your true emotion to them in your mind's eye, but only in a whisper. Place the talisman near a candle and a mirror which can just reflect a tiny ray of the moon's light. As the full moon arrives, your powers in love should prosper.

Full moon :
THIS IS THE FULL FACE OF THE GRACIOUS LADY MOON, ALSO CALLED THE ASTRAL MOON, WHICH RISES AS THE SUN SETS AND SETS AS HE RISES. The long, brightly moonlit night casts 'moonshadow' and is ideal for promoting astral travel and psychic dreams. This time embodies the psyche of opposites, turning things around, and invoking the greatest power of the mother moon, now in her zenith as maternal figure. The emotional highs associated with this moon have long been connected with mental imbalance (hence the terms 'moonstruck' and 'lunatic'). However, if you can balance your deeply enriched feeling power with your acute psychic awareness and inner consciousness, this is the moon to work the most powerful magic, to send messages far away and be telepathically at your peak. ❧ MAKE MAGIC FOR POWERFUL LOVE AND PASSION, OR TO COMMUNICATE WITH SOMEONE WHO IS AWAY FROM YOU OR NOT SPEAKING TO YOU AS YOU WOULD WISH. Reflect this 'below' (on earth) by putting scent on your pulse, lighting many candles and putting a photo of someone dear in the centre of them. Place an emblem of communication alongside – anything from a pen to a mobile phone!

Moon dreams :
IF THE MOON SPEAKS TO YOU IN SYMBOLS, SHE OFTEN SHOWS YOU FLOWERS. If you experience heavily scented flowers, you must grasp an opportunity that is offered you. If you see yourself gathering flowers, you will have a nice surprise, or be successful. If you see flowers gathered into a basket or vase, a new love is growing and you may hear of a wedding. If you see yourself floating over moonlit gardens, this is a general blessing and sign of luck.

Astral travel :
THE BEST SPELL TO DO ON A FULL MOON IS CONCERNED WITH ASTRAL TRAVEL. The bright moon is easy to see by, gives a lustrous daylight to the oddly-coloured landscape and inspires every part of our psyche, the liquid nature of our inner consciousness, heightening our perceptions and other-worldliness. This is something to do only if you feel comfortable and secure, for it is an exhilarating experience but can be unsettling the first time you try it. You will make good use of astral travel if you wish to find the answer to a problem, or to understand the nature of things unseen. You will be looking at the world about you from a completely detached perspective. ❧ THE OINTMENTS GIVEN HERE TO ENCOURAGE 'FLYING' OMIT POISONOUS HERBS THAT WERE ALWAYS USED IN THE PAST BUT WHICH ARE HALLUCINATORY. They were designed to increase the heartbeat and are dangerous to apply. I have substituted with some worthy successors for a less bumpy flight!

YOU WILL NEED

FLYING OIL ❧ *6 drops each of verbena, carnation, frankincense, sandalwood, musk or civet (synthetic)*
and patchouli oils mixed with 50 ml almond oil

WITCHES' SIGHT GRAINS ❧ *Powdered incense containing juniper, cinnamon or orange blossom*
in a pleasing blend, or a single note of one of them

A LIGHT TEA ❧ *1 tsp dried mugwort; 1 tsp vervain (verbena); 600 ml boiling water. Brew for 10 minutes, then strain.*

❧ FIND A WARM AND PRIVATE CORNER FROM WHICH TO 'TAKE OFF'. You need to stay warm during astral travel because you will experience the same drop in body temperature as when you sleep. Make sure you will be undisturbed – even by a cat. It is best to astral travel just before bedtime, when you can really immerse yourself in the experience and images and expand them. ❧ TAKE A SHOWER OR BATH AND THEN ANOINT YOURSELF WITH THE OILS, WHICH SHOULD BE APPLIED IN 13 PLACES UPON YOUR BODY: each ankle, the knees, your erogenous zone (but not internally), your belly button, breasts, wrists, base of the spine, and temples. ❧ LIGHT THE INCENSE, WHICH MUST BE PLACED SAFELY ON A HEATPROOF SURFACE AWAY FROM CURTAINS OR FABRIC. Drink some tea and address the moon, which ideally should be visible, or at least moonlight should be flowing into the room. ❧ NOW COUNT YOURSELF GENTLY BACKWARDS FROM 100, RELAXING YOUR BODY VERY SLOWLY FROM THE FEET UPWARDS AS YOU GO. Each time you pass a point where the oil is anointed (ankles, knees and so on), feel that part of your body really relaxing into a deep meditative state. Speak to yourself quietly in between every few numbers, saying that you are now relaxing deeply and will soon feel free and spiralling through the moonlit night where your mind can roam at will. By the time you reach your temples, you should be almost asleep, or only strangely conscious, but you will still be able to tell yourself that you will wake as soon as you wish to. The last words you hear yourself say should be: *"Now I shall fly gently over the rooftops in the dreamy night…"* ❧ AS YOU FLOAT, ASK YOURSELF VERY CALMLY WHAT IT IS THAT YOU WISH TO KNOW. You should have amazing images passing through your mind and may experience a genuine sense of 'lift off' and a feeling of being free from your heavy body. Either during the astral process or very soon after, when you retire to sleep for the night – which you should do without fully waking from the ritual of the travel – you will begin to experience vivid dreams or visual message sensations. When you have had enough, ask that you gently return to your physical self and recall all you have seen. When you wake, write up your key thoughts and memories in a moon-book or moon-diary.

Disseminating moon : THE MOON IS NOW ON THE WANE. Unlike the moisture-bringing waxing moon, this moon is drying, governing the ebb of the tides and of plant saps, so this is the time for harvesting crops and cutting flowers. The disseminating moon also takes away the extreme feelings of yesterday's full moon, the emotional tide gently ebbing away from the high pulse point. : THE MOON NOW IS VISIBLE FROM ABOUT AN HOUR AFTER SUNSET WELL INTO MID-MORNING, MAKING HER A GOOD CONFIDANTE FOR AN HONEST SELF-VIEW. Think of yourself, your direction, your present position and discuss this with the mid-morning moon over a cup of coffee. : NOW IS THE TIME FOR WORKING SPELLS OF REFLECTION AND DEEP THOUGHTS. On a physical level it is the perfect time to go on a cleansing diet or detox programme, as your body will not retain fluids as much as it does with the growing moon. If you have a one to two week healthy-eating regime planned, start on the disseminating moon and you'll be twice as likely to stick with it.

Waning half moon : NOW HALF LIGHT AND HALF DARK IN THE CIRCLE, THE MOON IN ITS LAST QUARTER WILL APPEAR AROUND MIDNIGHT AND BE VISIBLE WELL INTO THE DAYTIME, UNTIL ROUGHLY NOON. This is still the moon of reflection and meditative thought, but is used to work magic to rid ourselves of unwanted elements, which we demand to float away on the ebbing tide. Make circles in the early morning under the still-visible moon in a 'widdershins' direction (anti-clockwise). Turn your body thrice, pausing at each revolution. Carry a magnet and hold it away from your body. Invoke the negative element/virus/person to depart from you in peace. Present the magnet to the moon, then place it outside your house or near the front door of your flat, but hang it points down (not points up like a horseshoe whose luck you wish to preserve). Under the moon's darkness, in seven days, you will bury the magnet (see page 37).

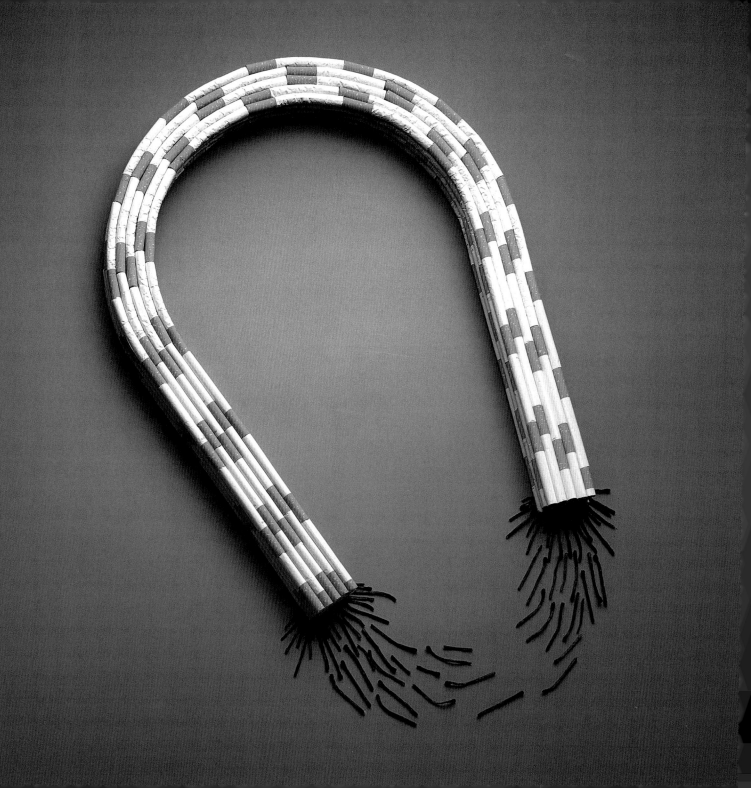

Waning crescent moon : THIS IS THE DAYTIME MOON, THE LAST SLIP OF MOON

SEEN EARLY IN THE MORNING, RISING JUST BEFORE THE SUNRISE AND NOT SETTING UNTIL LATER IN THE AFTERNOON. This moon, also known as the 'balsamic' or 'crone' moon, is almost dark and is dedicated to the crone or wise woman, who knows all from the darker worlds. She is the most mature and wise of the three-personed goddess: the maiden who was new, the mother who was full, and now the crone – the sibyl who sees both the future and deep into the hearts of men, knowing all, understanding what to change and what to leave be. This, then, is the moon of mystery and she watches over our rituals of divination and inner knowledge. She will help you to let go of things that no longer serve a useful purpose in your life – whether you want to give up smoking, quit a job or leave a lover! Look to the wise goddess face of the crone moon to understand unfathomed elements – to enquire of oracles or to direct your dreams to give the most complex and personal of answers.

Dark moon : JUST BEFORE THE NEW MOON APPEARS THERE ARE A COUPLE OF DAYS WHEN THE

MOON IS VIRTUALLY INVISIBLE. This is the dark moon, when it has waned almost away. Now is the time to turn completely inward and heal aspects of the self which require greater understanding. When we are in error, we need to think deeply and draw on unsilenced voices for an awareness of our obligations. This moment is apt to think on those dearest to us who have left us, to speak out to the ghosts of our past and wish them well, to place flowers on graves. Also, as this is the moon of the dark, we need self-honouring rituals to give us strength and confidence, for this is often the darkest personal moment of the month, 'the dark night of the soul, just before the dawn'. ❧ MAKE YOUR OWN MOON MAGIC NOW: sleep under a crystal, or find a round light with a moonlike shape which can lend us illumination. This is also the time to bury a magnet that has demagnetised negativity: this is the ritual you might already have begun (see page 34). Rid yourself of the bad feeling of a problem – such as illness or ill feeling from another person – by burying the magnet you have worked on for several days under a powerful tree such as an oak or an ash. Wish anyone involved in the bad feeling well, in another direction, as you go. Spend the last day of the dark moon in a personal reverie, quietly thinking, rather than being noisy and high-spirited – which behaviour belongs instead to (and should be elicited by) the full moon.

SOLAR
SABBATS

DEPENDING
ON THE DIFFERENT CULTURAL
FOCUS OF OUR ANCESTORS, THERE WERE TWO
KEY FESTIVAL CYCLES THAT DEVELOPED AS A BASIS
FOR WORK, THE CALENDAR, AND THE PSYCHE OF THE
PEOPLE. ONE OF THESE CYCLES WAS CONCERNED WITH THE
SUN'S PROGRESS THROUGH THE YEAR, ATTACHING GREATER
SIGNIFICANCE TO ITS MOST POWERFUL DAYS, WHILE THE OTHER
CYCLE FOCUSED ON THE MOON'S PASSAGE, THE SEASONS, AND HIGH
POINTS IN THE LUNAR CALENDAR. OUR FIRST CONCERN IS WITH THE
MAJESTIC POWERS OF THE SUN, AND THE DAYS THAT HONOUR AND
DRAW ON HIS POWERS. THIS IS MAGIC LINKED WITH THE DAWN
OF TIME; IT FORMS THE STEM OF THE WITCHES' SOLAR MAGIC,
THE FOUR SUN-RELATED DAYS OF THE EIGHT SABBATS.
BE ESPECIALLY AWARE OF THESE NATURALLY SIGNIFICANT
DAYS, OF THE BEAUTIFUL FLOW OF THE EARTH AND
THE SEASONAL PEAKS, AND OF OUR IMPORTANT
PSYCHOLOGICAL RESPONSE TO
THESE KEY DAYS.

The Spring Equinox :

THIS IS USUALLY MARCH 21ST IN THE NORTHERN HEMISPHERE AND SEPTEMBER 21ST IN THE SOUTHERN, THOUGH IT MAY VARY BY A DAY OR SO BECAUSE OF LEAP YEARS. On this day, the lengths of day and night are the same. ❧ UNDER THE MAGIC OF THIS MOMENT, WITH THE BALANCE EQUAL BETWEEN THE MOON'S INFLUENCE OVER EMOTION AND FEELING, AND HER RECEPTIVE POWERS, AND THE SUN'S INFLUENCE OVER OUR ACTIVE, PHYSICAL PERSONA AND OUR CONSCIOUS BEING, THE WITCH EMBARKS ON A MAGICAL JOURNEY. Male or female, now is the time to step forward into initiation. Here is one of the most beautiful purification rituals for self-initiation, designed to deepen your understanding and sharpen your focus on the world around you.

Shower with roses :

CEREMONIAL BATHING MARKS A DEPARTURE FROM AN OUTWORN PERCEPTION OR VIEWPOINT AND THE MOVE TO A NEW ONE. A shower has the feeling of spring about it, so you can make this a quick but profound personal statement. If you prefer the unhurried ritual of a bath, you can add in elements of your own thoughts that have personal significance. ❧ IN YOUR BATHROOM, CREATE A CIRCLE OF LIGHT MADE BY FIVE POINTS, USUALLY CANDLES, LOOSELY IN A STAR SHAPE. Use either a commercial shower gel based on rose, or make up one of your own using baby shampoo and a few drops of rose oil. Take also one real rose and, after you've showered but before drying, stroke the rose over your body, symbolising a new heightened awareness, a dedication to love and nature, and a declaration of innocence. Address the goddess and the god in your own words, expressing your intention to lead a magical life, asking for their blessings and guidance. Let your body air-dry as much as possible before you dress and step out of the circle of light. ❧ NOW WITNESS THE DEATH OF THE NON-WITCH BEFORE YOU. Find an old photo of you that you no longer like, or which was perhaps taken at an unhappy moment. Cover it in black paper or cloth and consign it either to the attic or the bin! Now you can assume a new name, which might be a nickname, or a middle name, or something completely new – or you may prefer to spell your own name differently to give it new resonance. ❧ NEXT, CREATE A PERMANENT CORNER THAT WILL BE YOUR ALTAR, PERHAPS IN THE GARDEN WITH SOME SPECIAL STONES. Address this with the witches' chant: *"I, (your new name), walk the path of the world now as a witch (or Wiccan, if you prefer)".* Celebrate your new birthday with cakes and ale (or tea, or juice), consumed in a circle of rose-scented candles, and share the bounty. You need never promise to do the bidding of anyone at all, but only to follow the rule to harm none and work only good magic.

The Summer Solstice: Midsummer Day ❧ This day

IS THE LONGEST OF THE YEAR, WITH TOTAL SUNSHINE IN THE ARCTIC CIRCLE. In the northern hemisphere this is around June 21st (depending on the year) and in the south it is December 21st or thereabouts. ❧ In days past, it was traditional to stay up all night on Midsummer Eve waiting for the rising sun, to celebrate the longest day of the sun's powers. Bonfires were lit and scented herbs and flowers along with little ritual gifts were burnt as offerings. Celebrations often included torch-lit processions and circles of revellers, with speeches to Fortuna, the lady of the wheel of fortune. The most important celebrations were held in circles of stone, where the sun was awaited for his magnificent heat and light from the earliest dawn. Marriages were performed at this time between couples who had pledged their unison at Imbolc (Valentine's Day) or Beltane (May Day). Jumping over small fires or wafting smoke were signs of purification and sharing the sun's power. ❧ Witches now work to capture the power of the sun. Evolve your own ritual with a mirror and a white candle – white being the colour of midsummer. Mirrors are sacred in magic for their intense reflective powers and because they capture symbolically the image of the ethereal light source. A ritual might include making a wish on a high place (a hill or even a tower), with a candle and a mirror glinting with the sun's light. Take time to notice and enjoy the day. Always make wishes for others, too, who need help in something. Leave a posy of simple summer flowers tied with ribbon on the summit after the wish, as an offering to the god and goddess who are symbolically married at high summer. This is why marriage is perfect for us at this time. ❧ The Summer Solstice is the peak moment for working magic ritual with standing stones, as at Stonehenge or Avebury. If you have none, you could create a mini stone-circle in your garden. Fill a cauldron with fresh flowers and water for a summer ritual, within the stone circle if possible. Most importantly, share the day with good friends and have fun, for this is the spirit of the solstice.

The Autumn Equinox : Check the exact date yearly — it will be close to

September 21st in the northern hemisphere, March 21st in the south. Daylight and night are once again balanced perfectly, opening our perceptions both to the daylight/obvious and the night-time/arcane. Our intuition and logic are in equal measure now, so this is a time for action rather than thought. The earth's energy is changing and we must respond to it.

❦ Fruits and grains are used in ritual; a traditional libation of cider or ale is often poured around the trees to bless their spirits and ensure their strength in the winter months. Pine cones, acorns and gourds are treated and varnished and placed around the house to ensure prosperity and repeated harvest, and to give thanks for present abundance. ❦ Whilst day and night are equal it is a ritual time, as at the spring equinox, for affairs concerning balance and harmony. This is the moment, then, to patch up quarrels, heal rifts and work on personal growth that springs from a balanced mind.

Rituals for peace and harmony : Early in the morning, make

up your own ritual centring it around symbols of peace and balance — scales, the symbols of Libra, or Yin and Yang, the olive branch, or anything else you like. This is a good time to make a talisman for peace and the ending of arguments by creating simple muslin sachets or little pillows from the herbs in your own garden — however small. Embroider together your own initials with those of people you care for and wish to see balanced with your energies. Fill the pouches or pillows with late September herbs such as lavender, rose petals, vervain, rosemary and mint. Keep one, and give another as a gift to your friend. ❦ To heal a serious rift, plant a little tree (even in a pot), putting paper slips with the names of you and your discordant friend under the tiny roots, then tend the tree to grow accord between you again. As at all solar festivals, end the day with some kind of social feast, with candles or a barbecue to honour the sun's changing mood!

The Winter Solstice : Midwinter Day in the southern hemisphere is June 21st,

though it hardly seems quite right to call it Yule, which has such wintry/Christmassy connotations. In the north, it is December 21st. Either way, it is the most important solar day of the year, as in some respects it marks the 'wheel' of the year, from which the word Yule hails. We are marking the shortest day and the moment of the sun's return, wherever you live! ❀ In the Pagan or Celtic past, it was considered very unlucky to turn any wheel on the day of Yule itself. First, one had to await the sun's own return, which meant a day of quiet and rest and honour. Perhaps these are the origins of our Christmas break (though this is hardly now a time of peace and quiet). However, this is a time to pause and think over the year, until the first signs of the lengthening day can be witnessed within a day or so. Then, we should look forward.

❀ The traditional burning of the Yule log ensures good luck for the coming year, but a piece of the log must be carried over until the following Yule. The Christmas candle, also of Pagan origin, was lit every night at the same time from Yule until January 6th to ensure luck and to encourage the return of the fire. As it was lit, the area of most need was uttered over it. Thus, in ritual, breathe a wish of most need – only one – over the candle as you light it from evening to evening. The tallow (or melted wax) should be kept and smeared on any implement of work – originally a plough or spade, but it might now be a pen or computer; this can be made to look pretty, as with sealing wax. You might equally take some of the fire's ash and put it around your winter-sleeping roses – a highly symbolic, but also utterly practical, gesture. Your roses will love it.

❀ Yule rituals can also include some reindeer talismans so that the horned god (Old Nick or Herne the Hunter) may personally attend your magic. Incorporate evergreens, which symbolise lasting life, into your altar or ritual; and again, create a fire-inspired feast to share with treasured friends or family.

LUNAR
SABBATS

WITCHCRAFT
WAS A NATURE CULT; IT FOCUSED
ON THE PROGRESS OF CROPS FROM SOWING
·TO GATHERING – USUALLY THE DOMAIN OF WOMEN –
AND ON THE MALE AREAS OF HUNTING AND HUSBANDRY.
EACH SEASON REQUIRED OBSERVANCE AND INVOLVEMENT WITH
THE SUN AND THE MOON, THE WEATHER AND THE RISING OF
RIVERS AND TIDES. THE LUNAR SABBATS ARE LINKED WITH THE OLD
AGRICULTURAL AND HUNTING SEASONS, AND COINCIDE MAGICALLY
WITH THE GREAT PHASES OF EARTHLY REINCARNATION – FROM DEATH
TO REBIRTH. THE FESTIVAL WE NOW CALL VALENTINE'S DAY WAS
ORIGINALLY KNOWN AS LUPERCALIA AND WAS THE CELEBRATORY
·MATING TIME OF ANIMALS (WHICH HAD TO BE PROTECTED FROM
WOLVES, HENCE THE NAME). THIS EVOLVED INTO A FESTIVAL OF
FRUITFULNESS, AND DEVOTEES WOULD DON ANIMAL SKINS
AND WEAR MASKS (STILL DONE AT CARNIVAL IN SOME
COUNTRIES), AND HANG SACRED TREES WITH
IMAGES AND SPELLS FOR LUCK, LOVE
AND FERTILITY.

Imbolc: the earth stirs ⁞ THIS IS THE FESTIVAL OF EARLY SPRING, CELEBRATED
ON FEBRUARY 1ST/2ND THE MOMENT WHEN THE EARTH RE-AWAKENS. This time magically belongs to the reappearing maiden goddess, full of sacred understanding from her time within the sleeping earth of winter. Nature heralds her return: the signs of life returning are not obvious, but they are apparent to those with careful sight, who will take the trouble to notice. The springs and swelling streams are her attributes – the life-giving waters of soul and survival. There are several significant rituals to perform.

⁞ CATKINS ARE NOW APPEARING ON THE TREES, ESPECIALLY WILLOWS, AND THIS IS THE TIME TO MAKE THE MOST IMPORTANT WISHES OF THE YEAR. On the first or second day in February, walk out to a willow tree (you should find one near a river or by water in a park). Tie a bow or a love-knot into a willow frond. Celebrate all joys and a rainbow of good feeling for others by attaching seven coloured ribbons of the spectrum in the pale green branches of the tree. They will flutter on the wind and bring prayers for goodness to all you think about. Only three precise wishes, however, are permitted during the year, so choose yours very carefully. ⁞ THE OTHER KEY RITE OF IMBOLC IS THE FESTIVAL OF LIGHTS, WHICH IS THE CHRISTIAN FESTIVAL OF CANDLEMAS. A circle should be made of candles or tea-lights and communion for higher inspiration should be sought from the goddess. As this is a lunar sabbat, there is a strong association with the mysteries of the unknown. Meditation at this time will bring enlightenment and clairvoyant answers, so it is appropriate to sit in a circle of lights, meditate, sing or chant, then ask questions of your inner soul that are troubling you. Answers come after a night's sleep, during which no word must be uttered. ⁞ AT THIS TIME ANY LOVE RITUALS WILL BE BEST APPLIED TO A VERY NEW LOVE, OR THE WISH TO MEET SOMEONE. The Imbolc maiden is innocent, but her senses are stirred and she is nubile. A shrine to love, harnessing the energies of Imbolc, will include attributes of femininity of the maiden: hair, ribbons and ornaments, as well as a simple vase containing a crocus or snowdrop. Honour to the maiden goddess at this time, incorporating the symbols of the flower and a lock of female hair, will bring blessings to all under the roof. Plant one white flower (such as a rose) at this time for peace and prosperity from the maiden.

May Day: the feast of Beltane ⁍ THIS IS THE MOMENT OF THE MAY:

both may tree and maypole spring from the powerful magic of tree worship. The maiden turns here from innocence to experience; this is the festival of sexuality. Once, for blessings and fertility, a may tree was planted in front of nearly every dwelling in the country. Those who couldn't plant a tree gathered green vegetation, beautiful boughs of flowers and greenery, and fastened them to the doors of their homes, bringing the providential blessing of the tree spirit. Traditionally, for powerful magical luck, the branches should be gathered after midnight on May Eve. Unbridled passion was completely endorsed at this time and couples would spend the night outdoors in the woods, testing their fertility. ⁍ ON MAY DAY ITSELF (MAY 1ST), ONE PERSON OF EACH SEX WAS ANOINTED WITH THE SPECIAL POWERS OF BRINGING 'GREEN' MAGIC INTO THE FIELDS AND THE HOUSES: they were the May Queen and the Green Man, also called the Whitsuntide King, Green George or Jack-in-the-Green. (His day was April 23rd and he was transformed in Christianity into St George, whose day is marked on April 23rd). ⁍ RITUALS FROM MAY DAY CAN BE BROUGHT ALIVE AGAIN TO EVOKE THE POWERFUL MAGIC OF THE PAST. For witches and Wiccans, these rituals include: the wearing of green; the purchase of a new tree and endowment with magic and spells as you plant it; the decking of boughs of green in the home, office and gardens, with ritual incantation for both personal fertility and communal fertility (prosperity); and/or the placing of a may wreath opposite the door or gate to avert bad weather. And most magically, the utilisation of the 'crack between the worlds' ushered in at Beltane – here, and at Samhain, there is the possibility of a glimpse into the fairy world. At this point winter is defeated by its rival summer, just as love rivals may go into battle for one prized heart wearing a token of birch leaves. ⁍ TAKE A PICNIC TO THE WOODS WITH THE ONE YOU LOVE AND 'OBSERVE SOME MAY REVELS'. Pack some body balms and massage oils to enjoy practise sensuality and flirting under your very own 'greenwood tree'. Lovemaking out of doors has always been condoned at this time, so be inventive, even if you're quite a private person. Magical ritual now is for the physical side of love.

Lammas: the feast of high summer ❧ LAMMAS, OR

LUGHNASADH, COMMEMORATES THE EARLIEST HARVEST TAKEN AT THE ZENITH OF SUMMER, AT THE END OF JULY OR

THE FIRST DAYS OF AUGUST IN THE NORTHERN HEMISPHERE (INVERT THIS IN THE SOUTH). Great magic made now must

be for career success, prosperity, material resolutions and protection. Be generous, but pay back debts. ❧ DRAWING ON OLD

MAGIC, PLACE A CORN DOLL IN THE GARDEN (OR ON YOUR DESK) TO ENSURE PROTECTION FROM STORMS. (This translates

to us as the placing of a lucky doll-object to ensure safe haven; it is still a custom to throw a doll of herbs or corn into flood waters

to encourage them to abate.) These storms may be metaphoric – the weathering of pressure at work, or difficulty in deciding what

to do vocationally. Cast your thoughts out on the tide with a small herb-crafted doll to attract powerful insights and to manifest

directions from nature and the gods. ❧ IF A BUSINESS OR COMMERCIAL IDEA IS LAUNCHED NOW, BUY OR MAKE A CHARM-

DOLL, DEDICATED TO THE GODDESS, TO KEEP AWAY PROBLEMS AND INVITE SUCCESS. Visit a sacred well or river to carry

your spirits into the realm of action rather than thought, and to effect healing or rest. Float flowers and herbs tied into a shape

in a fast-running river, asking for help and the creation of a signpost or direction for your future. ❧ ON A SOCIAL LEVEL,

LAMMAS IS THE TIME TO BAKE BREAD AND INVITE FRIENDS FOR A WISH PARTY. Birthday cake celebrations derive from

this – but the bread should be broken rather than cut. Crumbs should be tossed to the birds for luck and to thank the god and

goddess for providing. If it is a brilliant sunny day, take a long walk and mark the day properly. Make some connection with

grains (any grain, even pasta, noodles or couscous) for your supper.

Samhain: Hallowe'en : THIS FESTIVAL, THE OLD CELTIC NEW YEAR, IS STILL THE

BEST-KNOWN OF ALL, PRESERVING ITS MAGICAL AND RITUALISTIC FEEL THANKS MAINLY TO THE CELTIC PRESENCE IN AMERICA. Hallowe'en concerns magic and rituals of remembering the dead, being – like Imbolc – the moment when the 'crack' between the worlds of summer/winter and life/death is perceived as being open. : WITCHES STILL MAKE HALLOWE'EN A NEW YEAR CELEBRATION, WHEN MEMORY TURNS TO THE LOSS OF LOVED ONES IN THE PAST. Divination by all means is favoured now, so gather together friends and have oracle parties, look at horoscopes, or practise more traditional forms of divination. Appropriate witches' activities include scrying for the future through smoke or wax dropped in water, in both instances to discern shapes or letters. Nine candles are lit for the memory of friends and relatives departed, and a fire of nine sticks is lit for protection from prying but unwanted spirits. Apples should be woven into ritual, including one apple used in love spells. : IF SOMEONE YOU KNOW HAS LOST A RELATIVE, YOU MIGHT SUGGEST THIS PRACTICE TAKEN FROM DEEP MAGIC. Loving letters were once written and placed in the graves of the great warriors to read when they awoke in the immortal world. The ritual of writing letters to those with whom we have lost contact is both a comfort to the living and a magical thread of the unfinished words that will connect living and dead through the future. Spells for forgiveness and farewell can be written and placed in sacred places – under trees, or into fire, or even at a graveside.

The love apple : ONE OF THE LOVELIEST AND BEST-KNOWN HALLOWE'EN RITUALS CONCERNS

DIVINATION ABOUT LOVE FOR SINGLE WOMEN. Brush your hair in front of a mirror while eating an apple (symbol of the goddess of love) to bring a vision of your beloved: if the glow is soft and mellow the love is true; if the vision engenders fear, the love is fickle. It is particularly poetic – and some say accurate – if you create a mirror by filling a silver dish with water and perform this ceremony on Hallowe'en in the late evening. Often, the lover comes to visit or calls just after the ceremony!

SPRING

We now turn our thoughts to the seasons. While the festivals of the sabbats indicate particular energies on keynote days, each season has its gentle tasks and rhythms to be performed. In spring, we are inspired by the rebirth of the earth; nature is stirring, and the force fields of the earth are no longer apparently dormant. Magic worked at this time should draw on the extraordinary push for life and movement that can be felt after months of no activity. The witch now turns her attention to matters such as personal spring cleaning, as well as the practical tasks of sowing herbs and flowers that she will use in magic and healing throughout the year. And, most importantly, if you tune into the marvellous spring feeling of being alive again, magical things will be drawn to you in all spheres of your life. Element: air. Direction: east.

The heartbeat of spring : THIS IS THE SEASON OF OESTRE, GODDESS OF LIGHT

AND FERTILITY. Nature imbues us with teeming life; all creatures are brimming with sexual appetite and peak fecundity. From Oestre springs the festival of Ostara, renamed Easter by the Church. We still celebrate the potency of the egg as the symbol of renewal and the image of life waiting to burst forth – you will recognise this connection in the word 'oestrogen'. **THIS IS THE MAGICAL MOMENT FOR SPRING CLEANING.** Just as the trees begin to blossom, so may we. Our minds should be energised and our health and beauty flushed with optimism and vitality. Kick out all outworn premises and start from fresh anywhere your life seems jaded. **IT IS TIME TO USE THE BESOM, OR WITCH'S BROOM, FOR REBIRTH.** This is a symbolic act, but whipping up energy from this amazing symbol of fertility will really give you a buzz. Either make a broom yourself from birch twigs or strong herbs like rosemary, or ask a friend to give you one for luck; otherwise, you can use an ordinary household broom. Sweep through your home from front door to back, then out the front again, to rid you and your home from any doubts, anxieties and lack of confidence. When you have finished, face the east, direction of spring and the rising sun, and invite in a whole new determination and positivity. Put wind chimes or a hanging bell in the east to welcome spring and hear her voice. Place a carefully chosen stone, such as a gem or crystal, in an eastern corner of your house or garden: this will draw and radiate magic from the east. This is the first and most important act of the new spring. **TRADITIONALLY, THIS IS THE TIME TO PLAN AND LAY OUT A NEW GARDEN AND, IN PARTICULAR, A HEALING GARDEN, FOR THESE ARE THE ENERGIES OF SPRING.** If you are short of space, try to devote a kitchen window box to some of the following healing herbs: peppermint, sage, carnation, garlic, onion or chives, rue, lavender, marjoram or sorrel. Sow the seeds yourself if you want them to be especially magical. Your love and energy feeds the seedlings with an extra dimension of love, and thus magic. Any spells you wish to do which involve planting little herbs or shrubs should be done now. An excellent example is the one on the following page.

Magical tip: For general luck and health throughout the spring, tie coloured ribbons to the branches of some trees as they are veiled in their first green. Give each ribbon a wish, but remember not to be greedy. Make a little spring wreath for your front door in early March – just as though it were Christmas, but using spring flowers. Lady luck will soon come knocking.

A rite of spring: stepping from old into new

❧ "NEW LIFE IN AN OLD SHOE, I'LL BE MERRY WHATEVER I DO." Boots and shoes are an old symbol of prosperity and longevity. If boots were lost or toppled over, a miner might prefer not to work in the mines that day or a seaman not set sail for work. The idea of 'filling someone's shoes' is still used as a mark of having a long way to go to live up to another person's high qualities. ❧ AS A RITUAL TO WELCOME IN THE EARLIEST DAYS OF SPRING, CLOSE TO THE MOMENT OF IMBOLC (SEE PAGE 50), TRY THIS SOWING OF SPRING DREAMS.

YOU WILL NEED

Packets of mixed flower and/or herb seeds; an old pair of garden boots or clogs; soil; plastic film

❧ CHOOSE WONDERFUL FLOWERS FOR THIS EXERCISE, WHICH IS DESIGNED TO HAVE ALL YOUR HOPES GERMINATE ALONG WITH THE SEEDLINGS AFTER THE CHILLY DAYS OF WINTER HAVE PAST. Traditional seeds include love-in-a-mist (nigella damascena), lad's love (artemesia), kiss-me-in-the-buttery (pansy), maiden pink (dianthus), or summer savory (satureja hortensis), whose names reveal their potency for love potions and pouches. The very last, sown in spring and sprouting in June and July, is a favourite old aphrodisiac – sometimes called the 'herb of happiness' – and well worth growing. ❧ PACK THE BOOTS WITH GOOD SOIL, THEN SOW THE SEEDS LIGHTLY ON TOP OF THE SOIL AND SPRINKLE A FINE TILTH OVER THEM. Water gently, speaking your dreams of new projects (in keeping with the nature of spring) over them. Cover them gently with film and place them somewhere light and protected, where you can tend them with love. ❧ THIN OUT THE SEEDLINGS TOWARDS THE MIDDLE OF SPRING, BUT LET A FEW OF EACH CONTINUE TO GROW IN THE BOOTS WHERE THEY CAN FLOWER DIRECTLY. As the first seedling appears, make a wish and blow it to the east. As the first flower appears, pluck it with a wish and bring it indoors to a special altar, then press it in a personal book, locket or diary. ❧ WATCH YOUR DREAMS GROW INTO TRUTHS.

Ostara eggs ⁑ ONE BEAUTIFUL OSTARA CUSTOM IS THAT OF PAINTING, DECORATING AND MAKING

EGGS, WHICH SYMBOLISE THE LIFE FORCE. A willow basket of eggs is a traditional omen of luck and strength, and can be incorporated into your magic-making. ⁑ USE HARD-BOILED EGGS, WHICH CAN ALSO BE SYMBOLICALLY RETURNED TO THE EARTH AS PART OF A RITUAL. Choose wonderful colours to write, in tiny writing, little wishes and love spells on your eggs. Use pink to draw related images and write sweet words concerning a loved one. If you seek greater balance in a relationship, try drawing the scales, or the Yin and Yang symbol (see page 45). These images for peace in love are in keeping with the energies of spring balance, especially at the equinox. ⁑ ON OTHER EGGS YOU COULD PAINT BACKGROUNDS IN APPROPRIATE COLOURS: pink for love, blue for loyalty and stability, yellow for intellectual spark, red for passion, mauve for psychic activity, silver for feminine beauty, gold for money and green for health. Superimpose symbols of joy that are personal to you and those you love, perhaps hearts, letters, rings, flowers or clouds. ⁑ BE CREATIVE, AND MAKE UP YOUR OWN MESSAGES. Place the decorated eggs in a beautiful basket on an altar from late March through to early April, the first couple of weeks of the sign of Aries, symbolising action. ⁑ FOR A REALLY SPECIAL SPELL, YOU CAN 'BLOW' AN EGG. Make little holes carefully in either end of the egg, then blow out the contents very gently. Dip the egg carefully in glue and glitter, then decorate it with braids, threads, or ribbons, using the same colours given above to determine the area of spell. If you are very nimble-fingered you may be able to make a hole just big enough at one end to feed a tight scroll of rice paper into it, upon which you have written a worded spell with an incantation of love dedicated to the one you love. Do this in your own words, asking for the energy of spring to imbue new passion and power into a love affair. This would work particularly well on a not very physical relationship into which you would like to encourage more sensuality. ⁑ USING A VERY LONG NEEDLE, THREAD A LITTLE PIECE OF COTTON OR RIBBON THROUGH YOUR DECORATED EGG TO TIE IT TO A BRANCH OF A BUDDING TREE. Tie a knot in the bottom of the ribbon, perhaps with a bead or button attached, then hang the egg from the top. As you hang your egg spell face the east and ask the maiden to bless your endeavours, wishes and hopes with her most beguiling energies and powers of persuasion.

Spring love incense : THE THEORY OF INCENSE IN RITUAL IS THAT IT CARRIES

THOUGHT THROUGH THE ASTRAL PLANE, CONVERTING IDEAS INTO A MORE TANGIBLE ESSENCE. It also helps to stimulate intellectual and mental energy, sharpening our focus of thought for a while. We can both clear our heads of debris and open up a dialogue with the magical ether. ❧ A COMMERCIAL BLEND OF INCENSE WILL GIVE JOYOUS RESULTS; however, even more pleasure will be derived from making your own blend, controlling the elements you wish to awaken into thought, such as love, sensuality, positivity or success. Spring is the best time to make incense, partly because the senses are stirring, but also because spring rules the element of air, through which smoke must pass. Summer is also good, because of its association with fire.

YOU WILL NEED

½ teaspoon each ground cinnamon and cloves; 1 teaspoon powdered frankincense; a pinch of nutmeg;
1 teaspoon powdered dry myrtle or vervain leaves (the latter can be found as a tea at health food shops
and ground down in the mortar and pestle)

❧ I FIND A MORTAR AND PESTLE IS THE EASIEST PIECE OF EQUIPMENT TO USE FOR BLENDING INCENSE, THOUGH I KNOW SOME PEOPLE MUCH PREFER A BLENDER. Practise with both and see what works best for you. Gum resins such as benzoin or frankincense add cohesion to the other elements in incense and are easiest to work when they are cool, then ground with the other ingredients. ❧ WORK THE INGREDIENTS TOGETHER WELL. Depending on the temperature, you will get a gummy pellet or a more powdered lump that can be rolled into a pellet by dusting it with more sticky frankincense powder. To burn your incense you will need a charcoal burner, which can be found at most shops where you buy incense. ❧ PUT THE BURNER ON A HEATPROOF SURFACE, SUCH AS A STRONG CERAMIC DISH OR METAL CONTAINER, OR ON THE STONE HEARTH OF A FIREPLACE. Place the incense on the burner and light. Face again to the east, waft the smoke in that direction and offer up very simply worded (and unselfish) prayers concerning your desire for love. Breathe in the scent for about 15 minutes, then let the smoke drift around your home to draw love to your dwelling place. ❧ SPRINKLE ANY ASHES WHICH ARE LEFT OVER ON BUDDING PLANTS, ASKING ONCE MORE FOR A NEW BUDDING LOVE AND FOR JOY IN YOUR PERSONAL LIFE. As soon as you have performed this incense ritual, understand that the love vibration has begun somewhere in the astral for you. Leave it with good feelings and do not emit any panic or anxiety as to what will happen next. Just exude a gentle confidence that life has just begun anew. Keep spring flowers (even the smallest posy) in your home as you prepare for this love.

Rose-coloured dreams : To dream a prophetic and inspiring dream of enchantment that will awaken you with new beauty in the eyes of a loved one and excite their feelings for you. Make a brew of this delicious concoction before retiring to bed (whether or not you are alone).

You will need

*1 tablespoon fresh rose petals, or dried apothecary's rose; 1 teaspoon jasmine petals, or jasmine tea
(but fresh flowers are best); 1 vanilla pod; 1 stick cinnamon; 1 teaspoon fresh or dried vervain; a pink
china cup; 1 rose-scented candle; 1 drop benzoin oil in 5 ml carrier oil; 1 metre rose-pink satin ribbon*

❧ Combine the first five ingredients and pour over boiling water. Allow to brew for about ten minutes, then strain into a pretty pink or chintzy china cup. Before you sip, light the candle, massage your temples very gently with the diluted benzoin oil and tie the ribbon loosely around your waist. Sip, and think beautiful, romantic thoughts. The more strongly you can visualise, the more effective will be the spell. ❧ The tea will incite you to amazing, inspired, even quite psychic dreams, and you will wake with a look of romantic wildness and fresh beauty.

Conjuring salt : SALT IS A PRECIOUS AND POWERFUL COMMODITY, USED IN WITCHCRAFT

TO PROTECT AND CONSECRATE THE AREA IN WHICH YOU WORK, SUCH AS A CIRCLE. Control of the salt is also essential for survival and strength. Legend says that King Arthur's table was round so that every knight would be the same distance from the salt: the closer to the salt, the more favour and power one had. ❧ A DISH OF SALT OR SALT SPRINKLED INTO A CIRCLE OF PROTECTION WILL BRING THE MAGIC FORCE INTO LINE WITH THE ELEMENTS OF CREATION. Salt imbues the consumer with powerful sight and knowledge; it is said that salt shared between friends helps achieve likeness of mind. ❧ PERFORM THE RITUAL OF THE SALT AS NEAR TO THE SPRING EQUINOX AS POSSIBLE, PERHAPS WITH SOME FRIENDS, AS A PREFACE TO WORKING MAGIC FROM SPRING ONWARDS. On a sunny day, go somewhere close to running water – a river or stream, or the seashore. You could dedicate the salt to Diana, if you feel comfortable with that. ❧ AS NEAR AS YOU CAN MANAGE TO MIDDAY, TAKE A HANDFUL OF ROCK OR SEA SALT AND GO TO THE WATER'S EDGE; KNEEL BESIDE IT AND SAY:

"I conjure thee, great salt, to rest here in the stream of life and here at noon-tide; I cast my eyes to the sun and back to the water once more, that I may know my future, to prepare for what must be, and that I may gain control of all the irritations of my life that distract me from my path of mental calm and enlightenment. Beside the rising stream I take my place, and see the water round. And likewise I think on the growing sun, and in the water, sun and salt my soul finds strength, and asks the answers of great mysteries. Blessed be."

❧ NOW CAST THE SALT, ALL BUT A TINY PINCH, OUT INTO THE WATER AS AN OFFERING TO NATURE AND TO DIANA. Ask that you be given powers of discernment and wisdom, and that you may use these powers for the betterment of those around you and as unselfishly as possible. Finally, taste the remaining morsel of salt and consume it as a vow to careful thought, hard work and generous action. Bow a last time to these elements and say: *"Water, sun and salt, be gracious unto me"*. ❧ YOU ARE NOW EMPOWERED AS A HUMAN BEING AND READY TO WORK GOOD SPELLS FROM SPRING THROUGH SUMMER AND AUTUMN, BEFORE A RELATIVE PERIOD OF QUIET AROUND THE 'WHEEL OF THE YEAR' (AT YULE). 'Pinch' some salt and taste it before every important occasion.

SUMMER

XI XII I

X II

IX III

VIII IV

VII VI V

The

EARTH IS NOW LUSH WITH LIFE

AT ITS POTENCY, AND OUR OWN SENSES ARE

BRIMMING. WARM DAYS ENTICE SMILES IN THE SUN,

A RELAXED FEELING, THOUGHTS OF HOLIDAYS, AND THE

WISH TO BE OUTDOORS. NOW A WITCH'S TASKS ARE A

PLEASURE: TO PLANT A LOVE GARDEN RICH WITH ROSES, VIOLETS,

VERVAIN, LAVENDER, BASIL, LOVAGE AND PANSY; TO CREATE AN ALTAR

IN A HIGH PLACE; TO PLUCK A MAGICAL ROSE AT MIDSUMMER. THIS IS

ALSO THE APPROPRIATE MOMENT FOR THINKING OF WEDDINGS —

CALLED HANDFASTING CEREMONIES — WHICH ECHO THE MARRIAGE OF

THE GODS. IN SUMMER WE MAY 'CONJURE THE STONES' WITH A PIECE

OF CRYSTAL OR FOSSIL OR A SPECIAL GEM. IT IS CRUCIAL, AND

DELIGHTFUL, TO HAVE A COMMUNITY CELEBRATION OUT OF

DOORS DURING THIS TIME. AND NOW THAT YOU HAVE

LEARNED HOW TO MIX INCENSE, CELEBRATION INCENSE

IS FOR HIGH SUMMER, TO CAPTURE THE JOY OF

THE POWERFUL SUN. ELEMENT: FIRE.

DIRECTION: SOUTH.

A summer love garden : AT THE START OF SUMMER LAY OUT A GARDEN OF LOVE.

If you have been attentive you will have sown seeds in preparation for this in spring and will now have seedlings ready; otherwise you can buy established plants. It doesn't matter how small your potential garden space is – even if you only have a little window box or tub you can grow any of the following flowers to attract love and to perform love magic. ❧ LAVENDER IS EASY TO GROW AND WILL BE YOUR BEST FRIEND FOR LOVE POUCHES AND SACHETS AS WELL AS A HEALING PLANT. Varieties come in blue, mauve, pink and white in all sizes. If you have room for only one plant, make it lavender. A rose bush is essential, even if it must be a miniature. For love, choose pink and deep red shades, but always opt for scent. If you have space, old varieties in shrub form are indispensable for love spells and love potions. Delicate violets smell fabulous and attract love vibrations right to where you live; they have a short flowering season, but can be crystallised successfully. One tiny pot will provide hours of pleasure and a delightfully potent ingredient for pot pourris and especially love elixirs. As you tend your roses and violets dedicate them to Juno and Venus, the goddesses of female strength, allure and wisdom – you will have powerful allies. ❧ BASIL, LEMON BALM AND ROSEMARY WILL ATTRACT LOVE TO THE GROWER AND ARE POTENT INGREDIENTS IN MAGICAL SPELLS. And lastly, if you have space, sow borage and/or sweet peas – life will never be dull with these magical flowers around you. ❧ PLANT YOUR HERBS AND FLOWERS IN A PRETTY SHAPE: a heart, a crescent moon or a star will all add to the magic and will bring you astounding luck in your life – especially in love. If you desire fairy activity in the garden, place some crystals among the plants. I love to put little ribbons in between the flowers to bring rainbow happiness into the garden. Pots can also be tied with ribbons: pink to bring general love, red for passion, blue for loyalty. Harvest the flowers when they are in full bloom and either dry them for pot pourris or put them in glass jars for later use. Roses, lavender and sweet peas will scent sugar deliciously and you can then cook up love dishes with their fragrance.

Magical tip: Gather a few home-grown blooms and put them informally in simple containers beside a candle to entice the best feelings of love and joy from you and from the magical spirits around you. The simpler the arrangement the greater the power.

Conjuring the stones : STONES HAVE A SPECIAL PLACE IN RITUAL AND MAGIC.

Huge menhirs were placed for ritual in the great stone henges of our ancestors, and gemstones have been thought lucky and powerful for individual use in most cultures. Rocks and stones have knowledge of the earth and the past and the great climactic changes that have taken place long ago. When we borrow from their energies, we borrow from their wisdom and survival. In the Italian tradition of witchcraft, a stone found with any kind of hole in it was thought especially lucky, a mark of favour from the moon goddess Diana. ✻ WHEN YOU FIND A STONE IN SUMMER, EITHER ON THE BEACH OR THE ROAD OR SIMPLY IN A SHOP, PAY ATTENTION TO IT AND MARK IT WITH THIS RITUAL TO EMPOWER THE STONE AND ALIGN IT WITH YOUR OWN ENERGIES. Say: *"I have found upon my path today this holy-stone (originally a stone with a hole); I thank thee, Lady, for this lucky present, and the spirit which left it for me here; I charge it by the sun's great light to bring me luck and give me strength in adversity."* (At this, show it to the sun, and look through the hole at the sunlight). ✻ LATER ON THAT SAME DAY AT NIGHT, SAY: *"Tonight, by the moon's ethereal light, I charge it to bring me great fortune and deep thought. May its magnetic strengths give me the knowledge to draw to me those things that make my life complete."* The following morning, rise a shade earlier than usual and say, holding the stone: *"I rise in the early dawn, and through vales and meadows fair, or in towns and past houses, I walk with luck and knowledge to endure. All decisions I shall make now shall be wise. All friendships I make shall be strong. All paths I seek shall open to me."* ✻ Now THROW THE STONE UP TO THE HEAVENS THREE TIMES AND CATCH IT, THEN FINISH: *"I beg of thee, good spirit of the Lady, enter this stone and rest here in my pocket."* Always keep the stone in a safe place. ✻ YOUR STONE IS NOW SIGNATURE TO YOU AND MAGICAL, AND WILL BRING YOU STRANGE PROOFS OF LUCK. Use it in ceremony, wisely and not greedily, and thank the spirit of the Lady when you are granted your desires. Any stone found in summer is a holy-stone, and especially those with a hole in them, or that are completely rounded. If you are given a gem in high summer you may wish to dedicate it in this same way.

Flowers and herbs with magical properties

❧ HERE IS A GUIDE TO WHAT YOU CAN DO WITH THE FLOWERS YOU HARVEST DURING LATE SPRING AND SUMMER. Because summer sees the goddess at her marriage I have concentrated on flowers and herbs with special beauty options.

❧ SWEET VIOLET The beautiful scented flowers of this delicate little plant, white and mauve coloured, appear from late winter to very late spring. The scent whispers mystery but also innocence. So powerful is the fragrance that smelling the flower directly is only possible for a few seconds, after which the olfactory senses shut down for a rest and start again a moment later! The flower syrup treats coughs, headaches and insomnia – good for the night before an important day. The dried aerial parts of the plant also treat eczema and skin eruptions. Sweet violet was a well-known cordial for the heart, and a principal ingredient in many love potions. Try it in wine.

❧ LINDEN OR LIME BLOSSOM Here we have an untapped joy It has a wonderful 'green', grassy fragrance, and is a fabulous tonic for scalp, nails and hair. Like violet it treats nervous headache and tension as well as insomnia and is good for fractious children – try a mild tea. Cosmetically it has excellent properties for sensitive skin and is wonderful in a bath for muscular aches and pains. Men enjoy its honest fragrance too. It has the smell of a florist's shop.

❧ LILAC This is one of my absolute favourites. The scent is intense, rich, sweet and warm; one shrub can perfume the whole summer garden. Flower colours are particularly varied – mauve, purple, white and pink. The florets make a wonderful dessert garnish in food (try them just on ice cream) and the flowers and leaves cheer up a pot pourri. There is a close connection with lilacs as a 'fairy flower'. In simple bowls or vases they make one feel fey, ethereal and enigmatic – have them by when meeting a loved-one.

❧ ELDERFLOWER It is harder now to find these flowers on country walks than it used to be because so many are gathered to make the popular homemade cordial. Elderflower has an unusual green scent that would blend well with other florals in a vase for a love altar. As a light tea it aids hay-fever sufferers before the worst of the season, and the cooled tea also treats sore or tired eyes and an inflamed face – excellent for boys as an after shave. Magically, you need the support of the elder mother to be bewitching, so respect the flowers.

❀ ROSE GERANIUM Here is a scent that is well-known now, but the plant has some fabulous properties that are not so well understood. It releases its characteristic rosy-green smell, making it a favourite for perfumes and pot-pourris. Victorian skirts brushed against the leaves to release their scent. The essential oil is tonic, antiseptic, antidepressant and treats sluggish systems, cellulite, poor circulation and unbalanced skin. A drop or two in the bath refreshes and rejuvenates. It also magically protects against negative thoughts from others. Try some leaves in cooking.

❀ EVENING PRIMROSE Known to many for its powers of restoration after a heavy night-before, this is a wonderful hangover cure. We know what it does for menopausal or pre-menstrual tension, but it also helps to reduce eczema and feed healthy skin in capsule form. The flowers have a sweet honey scent and are magically very associated with women in control. Grow some in a pot – just to make you smile.

❀ HONEYSUCKLE A fragrant climber that is quite lovely and worth including even though it takes space to grow. The scent from its beautiful creamy yellow and pink flowers wafts through summer gardens, providing a mesmeric haven for humming bees on summer nights. The whole scent and headiness of the honeysuckle has been associated forever with romance and tenacity in love. The flowers (also called woodbine) yield a skin-softening toilet water with a powerful, trademark scent. The oil is quite expensive but is prized for cosmetic use, especially if the real thing (rather than a synthetic) is used. The twining flowers magically speak of loyalty in a relationship.

❀ GARDENIA This is another of my favourites and surprisingly, it is easy to grow in a small pot on a window sill. This talented and exotic flower treats nosebleeds, toothache and skin sores. The scent is balanced, like lavender and carnation – all have a perfect high, middle and low note. It is only ever needed, therefore, as a single floral note. Simply float the exotic blooms in warm water to release their sensual fragrance, or place a pot close at hand for a romantic summer evening supper.

❀ ORRIS OR IRIS Where to begin? This is a floral wonder and forms a magical ingredient in face packs, scented sachets, shampoos, body powders, and even tooth powders. It has a complex violet scent, used in soaps and perfumes. Iris was the flower of the goddess of the rainbow: in magic, a stem is synonymous with peace and feminine powers of persuasion.

❀ BASIL This lush-leafed and tasty plant is a favourite pot herb; it comes in rainbow colours, too. Its green leaves are

77

best-known, but purple and variegated varieties are interesting alternatives and the leaves of some varieties are lemon-scented. All are deliciously pungent when crushed in hot sun; the leaves steeped in wine are renowned as a tonic and aphrodisiac (sometimes one and the same thing). It is a top-note oil, with a sunny, 'light-green' fragrance, used as a smelling salt to revive our over-corseted female ancestors. Also antiseptic, tonic and a stimulant, the scent alone goads the tired brain into a flurry of focused ability; diluted oil or a very strong tea can be excellent as a foot-bath for summer feet. It should not be used during pregnancy. In Italy it is regarded magically as sacred to attracting love.

❧ Roses Ubiquitous in magic, these wonderfully sweet-scented flowers arrived, according to legend, with the birth of Venus, or Aphrodite, goddess of love. Magically, rose attracts love and protects lovers. It should be used in quantity to nurture a new love and equally to perpetuate a seasoned love affair. Always smell rose when you're under stress, or feeling emotional burnout, overwork, or any worries concerned with femininity. The goddess of the garden, its blooms in a vase are as magical as its petals in a glass of summer wine. Rosewater is inestimable as a gentle, soothing wash for tired skin, and good for people who are sensitive to many other products. It was used to fragrance the hair and put the goddess' own hand protectively on the heads of maidens courting love. Used after surgery, rose skin creams will speed healing. Rose works well for purification, to treat someone suffering from negative feelings, self-doubt or emotional disappointment. The cream is perfectly suited to treating drier or older skins, but sensitive skins also flourish on it. (See page 80 for a special summer rose ritual.)

❧ Jasmine This exotic immigrant needs no introduction. Its powerful, erotic fragrance is the favourite of many eastern countries. On warm evenings, the clusters of flowers on its elegant fronds emit a warm, narcotic scent. In love magic, jasmine was used in self-hypnosis to help the wearer assume greater powers of confidence and control than they might otherwise feel. The flowers may be tied into the hair for scent. The oil is very expensive, but a little goes a very long way. Cosmetically it helps dry, sensitive skins, corrects tiredness and is the best on offer for helping to overcome anxieties of a sexual nature. Not to be used at all in pregnancy, it is nevertheless excellent diluted as a massage oil during the birth itself.

❧ Madonna lily This fabulous fragrance is justly famous, and less sickly than other lilies. The flower yields an essential oil which is prized for perfume, and the summer bulbs have excellent cosmetic properties, particularly for ointments and for treating sunburn of inflamed skins. The distilled flower water, like rose and lavender water and orange blossom water, is a wonderful skin-toner. When infused with almond oil, it makes an excellent massage oil and counters eczema.

❧ TUBEROSE This truly exotic plant has lily-white flowers with an unbelievably intense, narcotic, sensual fragrance. It is one of the most expensive scents and oils in the world and its sensuous scent frees up recalcitrant lovers. Tuberose was so sacred it was used to fragrance the cool marble interiors of Italian basilicas. In Mexico, it enhanced the flavour of chocolate. Use in open spaces.

❧ LAVENDER If it were only possible to grow one magical plant, this would be it. Amongst its myriad attributes it is known for its power to bestow sensuality, clarity, confidence and humour, all or which qualities are induced as we inhale the perfume of this lovely plant. A sweet, cleansing but also relaxing fragrance, it is, like rose, the principal scent for pot-pourris, drawer liners, herb pillows, incense burners and dried flower bunches. A healthful drink and culinary aid, lavender cures insomnia, headaches and nausea and even eases halitosis as a mouthwash. Lavender water tones

the face, aids in cell renewal and treats acne. Magically, it is connected with overcoming depression or nervousness in love. Benefits to the mind and emotions are being tested, but it is associated with the bewitching powers of a woman – particularly women in their later twenties and over, who are no longer 'green' in love!

A Midsummer Night's rose : THIS ANCIENT RITUAL HAS FULFILLED THE
ROMANTIC DREAMS OF COUNTLESS YOUNG GIRLS. Why not try it yourself.

YOU WILL NEED

A white rose (picked as below); a sheet of white tissue paper; a white shoe box

❡ ON THE SUMMER SOLSTICE, AT THE CHIME OF MIDNIGHT, GO SILENTLY INTO THE GARDEN AND GATHER A WHITE ROSE. (If you don't have a garden or space outside you may have to cheat a little and find one.) Remember, this whole ritual must be done without speaking a word to anyone. Clasp the rose to your bosom and make a wish for happiness in love. Now walk silently backwards indoors and wrap the rose carefully in some clean, white tissue paper. Place it in a white shoe box and set it aside safely until Yule, or if you prefer, Christmas Day. On that day wear the rose pinned to your outfit (preferably a white top) and on that very day you should have a declaration of love.

A lavender ritual : ON LONG, LAZY, SUMMERY DAYS, WHEN YOU HAVE A HEADACHE THAT
SIMPLY WON'T SHIFT, A LOVED ONE IS TRYING TO TELL YOU SOMETHING! Try this ritual with lavender sprigs, preferably fresh from your own garden or pot (but dried will do).

YOU WILL NEED

1 tablespoon fresh lavender leaves (1 teaspoon dried); 600 ml boiling water; 1/2 teaspoon honey

❡ MAKE A MILD INFUSION OF LAVENDER TEA AND SWEETEN WITH HONEY. Brew for ten minutes, then sip the tea slowly, preferably outside. While you are drinking, ask who is thinking of you and what they wish to say to you. Look into the cup and you should soon see the face of your love, or someone else who is thinking of you. While you drink your tea, the message will come through, and your headache will evaporate.

Incense and marriage : SWEETLY SCENTED SMOKE SPIRALLING UPWARDS RITUALLY

HONOURS THE POWER OF THE SUN. Fire is involved in so much ritual, and incense is a simple way to bring this element into your magic. Both scent and vibration are released into the ether to carry thought. Nothing is more powerful for a ceremony of love such as marriage (or handfasting), as the smoke sends a message of serious intent to the heavens. It purifies and attracts the best spirit. ☽ HIGH SUMMER INCENSE COULD INCLUDE ORANGE BLOSSOM, WOOD AND PEEL; IT IS SACRED TO MARRIAGE, HONOURING THE UNION OF GODDESS AND GOD. Mix it on a Friday, sacred to love.

YOU WILL NEED

1 teaspoon powdered frankincense (sacred to the sun), which you have ground down from a lump in the mortar; 1 teaspoon rose petals; 1 teaspoon orange blossom flowers; 2 drops orange essential oil; 1 small piece orange peel, finely chopped

☽ MAKE UP THE INCENSE IN YOUR MORTAR AND PESTLE (OR BLENDER) WITH A SENSE OF CEREMONY, TALKING TO THE MIXTURE AS YOU WORK: *"I conjure thee, by Venus and Diana, to drive away what is not pure and happy, to rid us of doubt, and to be a blessing to the magic of love."* This incense is best burned on a charcoal burner and wafted through the area for love.

The handfasting ceremony : THIS IS THE WITCHES' VARIATION OF A

MARRIAGE CEREMONY. It will only be recognised legally if officiated over by a celebrant or officer with the power to conduct such legal ceremonies in their vicinity. The pledge is to last 'a year and a day', to be renewed on the same date twelve months hence. Usually the couples join their right hands, hand to hand, to symbolise their rational, male side; they then join left hands, joining their intuitive/female selves (see page 115). Seen overall, with both hands crossed over each other, this makes the symbol of infinity. Both parties may choose words that have individual resonance. Orange blossom, lilac blossom or rose petals should be strewn over the couple by friends, both as purification and as a magnet for strength in love and adversity. At the culmination, some couples may choose to 'jump over a broom' into the realms of marriage – but don't worry, this can be omitted if it feels odd.

☽ HANDFASTING SHOULD BE FOLLOWED BY A FEAST THAT INCLUDES THE CONSUMPTION OF ORANGE AND OF HONEY; so invite friends together if you are ready to make or renew these vows. June is the traditional month for handfasting, as it is the month of the oak, representing firmness of heart. The couple should be given a planted baby oak tree as symbol of their union.

AUTUMN

XII · I · II · III · IV · V · VI · VII · VIII · IX · X · XI

Autumn

PREPARES US FOR THE CHANGE FROM WARM TO COLD AS WE HEAD TOWARDS WINTER. THE DAYS ARE SHORTER AND COLDER, THE COLOURS OF THE LEAVES ALTER AND FRUITS ARE RIPENING, BUT WE FEEL INVIGORATED. FOR MANY, AUTUMN IS THE MOST VIVID AND WONDERFUL OF THE SEASONS, BEARING COMPARISON TO A GROWING PERSONAL MATURITY AND A DELIGHT IN THE RIPENESS OF LIFE. NOW IS THE TIME FOR COMPLETING OUTDOOR TASKS AND DRAWING INSPIRATION FROM NATURE'S MYRIAD ACTIVITIES. WE, TOO, CAN PLANT SEEDS THAT WILL DWELL ON THROUGH THE COLDER MONTHS AND GERMINATE AS PROJECTS THE FOLLOWING SPRING. MAKE AN EFFORT TO ACKNOWLEDGE THE HARVEST THIS YEAR – EITHER AT HALLOWE'EN OR THANKSGIVING. NOTE THE CHANGES, CELEBRATE THEM, AND RESPOND TO THEM. OUR SENSES AND ENERGY ARE HEIGHTENED BY THE BLEND OF SUNSHINE AND CRISP COOL WEATHER. ENJOY IT! ELEMENT: WATER. DIRECTION: WEST.

Herbal therapy :

TRY NEVER TO MISS THE MAGIC OF A MOMENT. At this time of the year, as the sap of trees and flowers returns to their root systems, we too are preparing to turn inward. Use these last magnificent days to prolong the joy of the harvest. ❧ GATHER IN YOUR LATE SUMMER HERBS AND MAKE HERB PILLOWS AND AMULETS FROM THE BOUNTY OF GARDEN AND HEDGES. Amulets are small pouches stuffed with different herbs chosen for love or success, into which some of your own magic words have been spoken. Cut lavender and rose for love pillows, mint to rid yourself of negativity, marjoram and rosemary for protection, lemon balm and basil for success in business. Make simple pillows or bags and give some as gifts. If you haven't enough of your own grown herbs, buy one or two pots and harvest from them.

Sparkling spirals :

AUTUMN IS THE PERFECT MOMENT FOR CELEBRATIONS WITH FIREWORKS. All the fire festivals were held at this time and Hallowe'en, replaced in Britain by Guy Fawkes, preserves the lighting of beacons and ritual of coming together for pyrotechnic delights. Make a cake and place sparklers – representing the spark of energy – on top rather than candles. Or set out a tiny altar in the garden using outdoor candles, wind chimes and spirals, for these are the symbols of autumn. The spiral shows the earth's energy coiling itself for retraction and then re-launching. Autumn, like spring, is a season of balance between light and dark, warm and cool – your garden altar could reflect the balance shown by the scales in the sign of Libra. Wind chimes recall the power of the westerly winds of autumn, so even if you only have a tiny space in the city to live, hang wind chimes in the window to usher in melodically the magic and power of the west wind. ❧ THE ELEMENT OF AUTUMN IS WATER, SO OFTEN DEMONSTRATED BY THE RAINS WHICH RETURN AT THIS TIME. Place some pebbles in a dish with some sand and water, or grow something hydroponically. Add a sparkler instead of a candle, and honour the fire ceremonies. Make a wish as you light it and envisage your goal achieved.

Growing spells :

BULBS ARE STRONGLY MAGICAL. The numerous layers enfolded in their skins seem to represent humanity, thus they have a long history of use in spells. Autumn is the time to begin a ritual with bulbs, partly because they should be planted now to over-winter and bloom in spring, but also because of the symbolism of something new generated from something old. During the winter months ahead, while the bulb sleeps and prepares to unleash its life in the spring, it is close to the secrets of the unknown, taking its strength from the dark realms. This will imbue the speller with extra powers of hidden wisdom.

You will need

A medium sized pot; 1 or more bulbs (tulips, hyacinths, daffodils, amaryllis lilies, or even little snowdrops, crocuses or grape hyacinths); bulb fibre; a tiny sheet of paper; 1 emblem of love or success (such as a coin, heart brooch or other charm)

CHOOSE A REALLY PRETTY POT TO COMPLEMENT YOUR CHOICE OF BULB/S. Make your colour choice of flower count; yellow would be more suited to money spells, whereas pinks or reds suit love. If you wish to start over again in love, because of breaks or bad luck in the recent past, choose a white flower. If you want a more exciting life/career etc, choose an appropriately exotic bulb. Choose something scented, like a hyacinth, if you want to transmit thought to someone a long way away. WRITE A LITTLE NOTE OR SPELL IN YOUR OWN WORDS, KEEPING THEM SIMPLE, THEN PLACE YOUR SCRAP OF PAPER AND THE CHARM DEEP IN THE SOIL IN THE POT. Plant your bulb/s above and tuck the remaining soil around. As you water the bulb after planting, say: *"May I, too, nurture my inner self, and emerge like a butterfly in spring".* COVER THE POT WITH DARK PLASTIC, AND PLACE IT SOMEWHERE COOL. Remove the plastic after about six weeks, near to mid-winter, then speak loving words to it every day for several weeks until the green shoots look strong. Your area of interest will be gradually sprouting too and, as the bulb flowers, your life will blossom anew.

The magical spiral of strength ⁏ THE SEASON IS SPIRALLING TOWARD

ITS WINTRY REST. Life is ebbing, and this can be a very happy experience, turning inward to hear your own needs. The spiral is a very positive symbol, ancient in Celtic magic, sacred to the idea of descent into periods of test and trial, with a safe return. Like Ariadne in the labyrinth in the ancient Greek legend, holding onto the thread means we are safe in the knowledge that we can come back again. ❧ ONE OF YOUR SEASONAL TASKS IS TO EMBROIDER OR MAKE A SPIRAL. This may be contrived from cottons or ribbons, in the garden with stones, or you may choose to weave a basket to emblematise the move through new knowledge and tests of your strength. If you have no confidence in your powers with the needle or in weaving, try simply drawing an elaborate spiral, possibly writing your own words of spells and incantation in between the lines. In the making of it, you will gain a powerful tool that will enable you to rise above adversity. No matter how others test you, you will still know where you are bound. The spiral reminds us that most demands in life are tests of the strength of our minds – our recovery of optimism, of will, or our capacity to find a way around obstacles with cheerful determination. ❧ YOUR GARDEN SPIRAL COULD BE LAID WITH STONES LEADING TO A CENTRAL FEATURE – A POTTED PLANT, A WATER-FILLED VESSEL OR EVEN A SYMBOL OF RE-ORIENTATION SUCH AS AN ARMILLERY SPHERE, A SUNDIAL OR A COMPASS POINT. Plant the spiral with little crocuses, snowdrops or other early bulbs, to give you strength and powers of recovery as well as luck with the first signs of spring. ❧ IF YOU EMBROIDER A SPIRAL, CHOOSE MAGICAL COLOURS: pink for love, red for passion, green for health, purple and indigo for spirituality, blue for protection. Weave in little tiny symbols – hearts, flowers, shells, keys, coins or a house. According to your choice, you will be able to overcome tests in any of these areas. The spiral is your lucky compass point, ever pointing you back towards home.

Magic from the autumn garden : NOW IS THE TIME TO USE THE

LAST CROP OF LAVENDER. Harvest any remaining flower stalks, use the flowers and leaves in herb pillows, tie the rest up in bunches and hang up to dry in a warm place. Lavender can be kept like this for months, scenting rooms throughout the winter, or made into little sachets for the linen cupboard and your drawers to introduce magic and love amongst your personal things. Lavender is also a crucial ingredient in pot-pourri. Use your autumn lavender with vervain for a potent love pot-pourri for the bedroom. Before you go to bed, stir it with your left ring finger and ask your dreams any question concerning love affairs. You will be directed to the answer as you sleep. ❧ BORAGE, A VITAL INGREDIENT IN SUMMER LOVE POTIONS, IS A WONDERFUL DIVINATION HERB IN AUTUMN. Its prolific and beautiful blue flowers appear right into the coldest weather, lasting until the frosts. Place one flower on your forehead with your index finger, light a candle of the same blue and ask a question concerning your fate. You should soon receive the answer. A flower can likewise be pressed into a book of divination, such as an oracle, or a pack of tarot cards. You will get even clearer insights and should keep the flower there. ❧ ROSE HIPS SUCCEED THE FLOWERS IN MANY AUTUMN ROSES. Collect and make a light tea with them to soothe your spirits when you need to find solutions on a day of headaches. Inhaling rose oil at the same time will make you feel wiser, more forgiving of the world around you and able to cope with tension. ❧ YARROW STALKS HAVE A HISTORY OF USE IN DIVINATION. If you have space to grow this aromatic plant, remove the foliage in autumn and retain the stalks in a pile. Ask a question requiring a 'yes' or 'no' answer, close your eyes and sweep the pile into two roughly equal heaps, then count them. Those to your left say 'yes', and those to the right, 'no'. The greater number in either pile will give the result. ❧ A FINAL METHOD OF DIVINATION FROM THE AUTUMN GARDEN IS TO PLANT AN ONION WITH A QUESTION WRITTEN BELOW. If you cannot choose between two or more possible paths, plant onions in the early autumn. For each possibility – such as wondering which lover is truer, or which course to take, or which home to move to – put the name of each of your two choices under an onion bulb in a blue pot. Whichever bulb shoots the first true green shoot will be your strongest option – but it is worth observing the shoots for a week or more, to see whether an early winner shows signs of being overtaken by a rival for strength and beauty.

Conjuring the wind :

WITCHES HAVE EVER BEEN ASSOCIATED WITH POWER OVER THE WEATHER. In Britain, where the climate is so changeable, I have confined my own spells to requests for sunny bursts in between bad days, even in summer. I usually manage to get away with a barbecue on a fixed date, or the clouds clearing for an outside occasion just long enough to make a good photo or reach the car. ❧ THE CONJURING OF THE WIND IS AN OLD CUSTOM, PERFORMED IN AUTUMN WHEN THE WIND HAS THE JOB OF CLEARING AWAY THE PAST AND PREPARING FOR THE NEW. Raising a wind will rid us of depression or apathy, or even purge ill-luck. Traditionally, a wind might be conjured up to enhance the chance of escape from trouble. In the tale told me by my grandmother, which bears a close resemblance to some of the features of Keats' Ode to Saint Agnes, it facilitated a young girl's escape from confinement to the arms of her lover as the house around her, in Volterra in Italy, actually blew down. It might be best to stop the spell before you achieve a tempest such as that!

A spell to blow away ill fortune :

GO TO AN OPEN SPACE SUCH AS A GARDEN, A PARK, OR BY WATER IN THE EARLY EVENING AND LOOK UP AT THE MOON. You may use your own words, but your invocation should be somewhat along these lines: *"Gentle Diana, I am presently feeling heavy and oppressed* (you might express the reasons why) *and ask of you a sign of change in my situation. Let me scent the air of change, and send me a breeze, gentle as the zephyr, or a wind, powerful and commanding, to blow away the sadness and restraint that I feel."* Sprinkle a little salt on the ground and a few drops of water from a little flask or bottle. Look up again at the moon and say: *"Lovely goddess of the bow, lovely lady of the arrows, raise up your hounds, and hunt away my woe"*. You should leave one moon-coloured flower, crystal or gem in the place where you have stood. ❧ DURING THE COURSE OF THE EVENING THE WIND SHOULD BEGIN TO RISE. Do not be surprised, indeed, if a storm may appear that lasts for a day! Make sure you feel at least some of the wind through your hair, and if rain comes, let it wash away your uncertainties. ❧ NOW, THE TIDE IN YOUR LIFE MAY CHANGE, AND YOUR LUCK TURN FOR THE BETTER IN ALL THINGS.

Protecting love : AUTUMN IS THE APPROPRIATE SEASON IN WHICH TO PROTECT THOSE WE

WANT TO COME HOME SAFE. The spell below is applicable whether you have a love going away for a while, or a new love who you want to protect. Put your heart and soul into it.

YOU WILL NEED

A few fresh or dried flowers; an autumn leaf in full colour (yellow or red-orange); a small flower frame; coloured ink; rose oil

❧ BEGIN BY CHOOSING YOUR FLOWERS, DEPENDING ON WHAT YOU WANT TO SAY. Autumn flowers available would include michaelmas daisy (*"I wait for your decision"*), geranium (*"I can wait for you"*), honeysuckle (*"I send you a token of my love"*), hyacinth (blue: *"I dedicate myself to you"*, or white: *"I esteem you greatly"*), cyclamen (*"We will overcome difficulty"*), tiger lily (*"I am passionate about you"*), myrtle (*"I am forever true to you"*), pansy (white for kind thoughts, yellow is *"Oceans part us"*, purple for deep love), rosemary flowers (*"I always remember you"*), guelder rose (*"Autumn love"*), wallflowers (*"Constancy through rain and storm"*). An ash leaf added brings lion-like perseverance; an oak leaf brings courage; holly (*"We will be restored to one another"*); poplar (*"All will turn out well"*); maple (*"Do not leave me from your thoughts"*); and willow (*"My weeping will end"*). Clover added will bring luck and protection. ❧ PRESS YOUR FLOWERS AND LEAVES INTO A PRETTY ENSEMBLE, THEN WRITE A TINY MESSAGE BETWEEN THE LEAVES AND PETALS IN BEAUTIFUL COLOURED INK, WHICH YOU HAVE SCENTED IN THE BOTTLE WITH A FEW DROPS OF ROSE OIL. If you wish, write out the meanings of the flowers you have chosen. At the bottom, just under the press frame, write your name with your loved one and the year in Roman numerals. When the frame is fully ready, hang it somewhere it will catch the light. ❧ YOUR LOVE WILL NOW GROW STRONGER IN PROPORTION TO THE STRENGTH OF YOUR OWN FEELING AND YOUR ABILITY TO TRUST YOUR PARTNER.

WINTER

From
THE MOMENT AUTUMN BEGINS
TO EBB AWAY WE ARE ONLY TOO AWARE THAT
THE DAYLIGHT HOURS ARE SHRINKING AND THE
EARTH IS WITHDRAWING INTO ITSELF. ALL THE ENERGY OF
THE EARTH'S LIFE FORCE IS DRAWN BACK INTO THE ROOT
SYSTEMS, AND WE MUST USE THIS SEASON TO DO THE SAME. WE
CAN TURN INWARD, INTO OUR OWN DREAM WORLD, TO EXPLORE OUR
UNCONSCIOUS AND DEEPEST DESIRES, WHICH CAN THEN BE TURNED
INTO A STRONGER REALITY IN THE SPRING. THIS IS THE TIME TO
SOOTHE, PROTECT AND HEAL OUR SPIRIT, WHICH OFTEN FEELS SORELY
TESTED WITHOUT THE SUN'S POWERS IN SUCH FULL FORCE. THIS
PERHAPS IS WHY THE MOMENT OF YULE, MIDWINTER DAY, WHEN
THE SUN HITS ITS SHORTEST POINT AND BEGINS TO TRAVEL BACK
TO US AGAIN, IS PSYCHOLOGICALLY SO IMPORTANT. BUT FOR
THE NEXT FEW MONTHS, IN OUR HOMES, GARDENS,
HEARTS AND SPIRIT, WE MUST MAKE SURE WE
'RUG UP WARM'. ELEMENT: EARTH.
DIRECTION: NORTH.

Winter warmers :

THE PRIME EFFORT OF MAGICAL ENDEAVOUR AT THIS TIME IS TO BRING INTO OUR TERRITORY REMINDERS OF THE STILL-PULSING LIFE FORCE, SO THAT WE CAN KEEP OUR LOW BATTERIES CHARGED JUST ENOUGH FOR SURVIVAL AND TO EDDY OUR MOOD UP TO A HIGHER POINT. This was the reason behind bringing in evergreens to the house and the table. Pine, mistletoe, ivy and holly, which had such a significant magical ritual function throughout the seasons, are now called upon to impart their message of strength in adversity, representing as they do everlasting life. ❧ TEND YOUR MAGICAL GARDEN AT THIS TIME. Bring in any herbs in pots, to shelter them from the worst of the weather. If your garden is more substantial, cover herbs and flowers with proper glass cloches, sheets of plastic or straw for protection. But you can also generate magic in your garden, for all is not dead. This is the moment to clip your bay tree into pretty wintry shapes – stars, or spheres, or anything you please. Chant a spell while you work, because bay is sacred to Jupiter and any cosmetic work you attend to on a sacred tree brings the favour of the gods. Ask favours that are in his domain: entertainment, a little extra prosperity, help with learning, travel or law. Place a little walnut under each tree when you finish the wording of your spell-wish. ❧ TIE RIBBONS TO THE BRANCHES OF BARE TREES AND PRETTY UP YOUR FESTIVE GREENERY WITH RIBBONS OF ALL COLOURS. Choose appropriate colours for your hopes for the year ahead – pinks and reds for love and passion, greens and blues for security, health and protection. Under one special tree, perhaps the one you like the most, or one which was planted for a special reason, place an outside candle in a weather-proof holder. Light it for an hour or so, saying personal things to someone who is (for any reason) out of reach but in your heart. Tell your most private wishes and desires to the earth itself, whose element belongs to winter. Afterwards, be still for a few moments. This is a time to listen acutely to the almost inaudible breathing of the earth and of your heart.

Conjuring the horn of plenty : This ancient ritual is connected

WITH SUNNY CLIMES WHERE THE GRAPE IS PART OF THE STAPLE OF ECONOMY AND JOY CONJOINED. It bears a close
resemblance to the wassail ceremony in the north, with the apple trees honoured on Twelfth Night Eve. You could perform this
if you or a friend have a grapevine growing; otherwise take grapes and a horn of wine yourself and go into a garden area, enacting
this symbolically at any tree. The wine itself should be a pleasure.

The vineyard ritual : When you wish for a good harvest, go in winter into

THE VINEYARD OR WHEREVER VINES MAY GROW, ON A WAXING MOON. Look up to the lady of the moon and ask of Diana her
help and favour with your future prosperity in this way. Charging your 'glass' or horn, toast the moon, saying: *"This is no ordinary
wine I drink, but the essence of your life and energies. Diana, spread the vitality of the wine into my vines, and may the grape and my
fortunes ripen in the waxing moon. I kiss the hand of the Lady of the Growing Moon, and from this day, until the first bud appears, and
the fruit indeed ripens, I ask your blessings on my house. May I draw in equal measure, profit and pleasure with friends and loved ones."*
(Pour a little wine into the ground around the vine or tree). *"I salute here the horns of the moon, with the horn of Bacchus, and
promise to balance work and rest-time, responsibility and merriment, in equal proportion."* Now you should cast a few
GRAPES AROUND THE BASE OF THE TREE OR VINE, BE STILL FOR A FEW MOMENTS AND THINK OF WHAT A 'PROSPEROUS
HARVEST' MEANS FOR YOU INDIVIDUALLY. Keep some grapes on your main table or at a simple altar for the remainder of the
moon, right through the waxing process until it has waned and appeared new. The grapes may be eaten, but must be replaced.

Winter incense : THIS IS A KEY TIME FOR THE BURNING OF INCENSE. Always an aid to

meditation and inward thinking, the smoke also recalls the scent of the growing trees and resins, rejuvenating the wintry air with life and magic. Blend your own incense if you can, otherwise choose ready-made incenses with which you can work magic and utilise in unusual ways. **:** THE RESIN MUST MAKE UP ABOUT HALF OF THE MIXTURE. You may choose to add a touch of sugar, which will sweeten the scent and appease the magical spirits, who adore the sweetness in the air. Frankincense is a wonderful choice for scenting linen and bedding as well as rooms, for it adds a blessing to the necessaries of daily life in the winter. A sacred blend would have been three-quarters frankincense and one-quarter myrrh. Blend your ingredients with your mortar and pestle before weighing the quantities.

YOU WILL NEED

½ teaspoon frankincense; ½ teaspoon pine needles; ½ teaspoon lemon or orange peel; 1 bayleaf;
a tiny slice of cinnamon stick; a few grains sugar

: BLEND ALL THE POWDERED INGREDIENTS TOGETHER, LIGHT A CAREFULLY INSULATED CHARCOAL DISC AND PLACE YOUR INCENSE ON IT WHEN THE HEAT HAS TURNED IT GREY/RED. Waft the smoke towards your linens and into your dining area. Ask for resilience and triumph over winter ills and seasonal irritations. Very quietly, honour the essence of the sleeping earth. Imagine the incense circling around your home and protecting all that is in it. Stay very calm and quiet, enjoying the scent, while the fragrance lingers – approximately one hour. It will brighten your mood, add confidence and zest, and enhance your mental vigour.

Spell ribbons :

THERE IS A VERY SPECIAL RITUAL TO BE PERFORMED WITH RIBBONS IN WINTER TIME, WHEN THEIR COLOUR IS SO IMPORTANT IN A BROWN-GREY WORLD. Try this. ❧ PURCHASE SOME REALLY BROAD RIBBON, 2–3 CM WIDE, IN PINK FOR LOVE OR BLUE FOR LUCK. Take a contrasting coloured thread and very carefully embroider your name or initials into the ribbon. By early, waxing moonlight, take the ribbon to the prettiest bare tree – one with a perfect shape. Ask la donna de la luna (the lady of the moon) in her wintry brightness, the sole luminary of the winter sky, to favour your dearest hopes (in love or in luck) with her magical touch. Tie the ribbon securely into the tree. For the remainder of the moon, wear a stone such as a moonstone or milk opal or a very white diamond, in honour of the moon. Before winter is ended, you will be lucky in your hopes.

The winter wreath :

THE MAKING OF A YULE WREATH IS AN AGE-OLD TRADITION, INSEPARABLE FROM THE IDEA OF CHRISTMAS ITSELF. However, for your winter spell-making create a separate wreath which can be used in the days up to Yule or from January until spring. It is a symbol of life returning, encouraging the very world to turn – even including your own private world. ❧ TO MAKE YOUR WREATH, YOU CAN USE WIRE AS THE BASE, ALTHOUGH WILLOW OR HAZEL IS TRADITIONAL. Take several lengths of willow or hazel, each about a metre in length, and wrap them around into a circle, weaving the tail end around the main circular shape to create a full thick circle. Start anew with each piece weaving in over the old, securing with little pieces of green thread or ribbon if you need to. Now add in some fragrant stems, such as rosemary, lemon verbena or thyme, weaving them around the circlet and again securing in place with ribbon, wire or thread. Finally, cover the frame with evergreen herbs like bay or box or pine, overlapping each piece with another, binding with ribbon or wire as you go. Make sure all the branches face in the same direction. Now wire or tie in some berries, dryish winter flowers or pine cones sprayed gold. Keep one wish foremost in your thoughts as you work your wreath. ❧ WHEN THE WREATH IS READY, TIE IT INTO PLACE ON AN INSIDE DOOR OR LAY IT FLAT IN THE CENTRE OF A TABLE. Promise to be true to your wish for the year's length and expect a pleasing resolution, indeed, within the year.

The winter ironing basket :

IRON IS VERY IMPORTANT IN MAGIC AND WAS ONCE REGARDED AS SACRED TO THE GODDESS EPONA OF THE MOON AND HORSES, THE CELTIC DEITY EQUIVALENT TO DIANA, WHO IS REVERED IN WITCHCRAFT. Iron is a powerful metal that stores the knowledge of the 'dark world' – which means not evil or negative magic but that which is hidden from us, in the realms where the earth sleeps. This is a product of the womb of Mother Earth. ❧ A WONDROUS WINTER TASK RECALLS THE MAGIC OF IRON; IT IS CONNECTED WITH THE OLD-FASHIONED PRESSING IMPLEMENT, REMINDING US THAT IN THE PAST IRONS WERE INDEED MADE FROM IRON. The process of scenting your linen at this time of year with the aromas of the summer months buffets your sinking spirits and wafts gladness into the psyche. Don't underestimate the importance of the task nor the lovely result of fragrancing your clothes in this way. When roses and lavender are diluted into distilled water for the ironing, you are indeed recalling the energy of the sun and producing magical effects from the iron itself. By all means use commercial linen sprays, but if at all possible make your own, for no commercial product quite reaches linen kissed in winter by your own preparation. ❧ USE 5 DROPS EACH OF ROSE AND LAVENDER OIL WITH 3 DROPS OF ROSEMARY OIL AND 2 DROPS OF BERGAMOT OIL, ADD TO 50 ML DISTILLED WATER, BLEND WELL AND ADD TO THE WATER CHAMBER OF YOUR IRON. The resulting scent will help to counter cigarette smells, laundry chemicals and bacteria, and will lift your spirits majestically above the grey winter skies. If you are ironing for a love date, increase the rose quantity to 8 drops and omit the rosemary. There is a real property in these flower oils, but a magical one too. All of them heal magically and all attract 'butterflies' in the best sense: in other words, the goddess attends you. Always iron your clothes or linen in this way on an important day/date for luck from above – and add a pink ribbon around the handle of the iron if you are meeting your lover. ❧ YOU CAN BOOST THE IRON'S GIFTS WITH A SWAG MADE UP IN LATE AUTUMN FROM THE LAST ROSEMARY AND LAVENDER. Tie it with a purple ribbon and hang it upside down in your linen cupboard, where it will discourage insects as well as negativity. Always scent your sheets in this way if you like to sleep with romance.

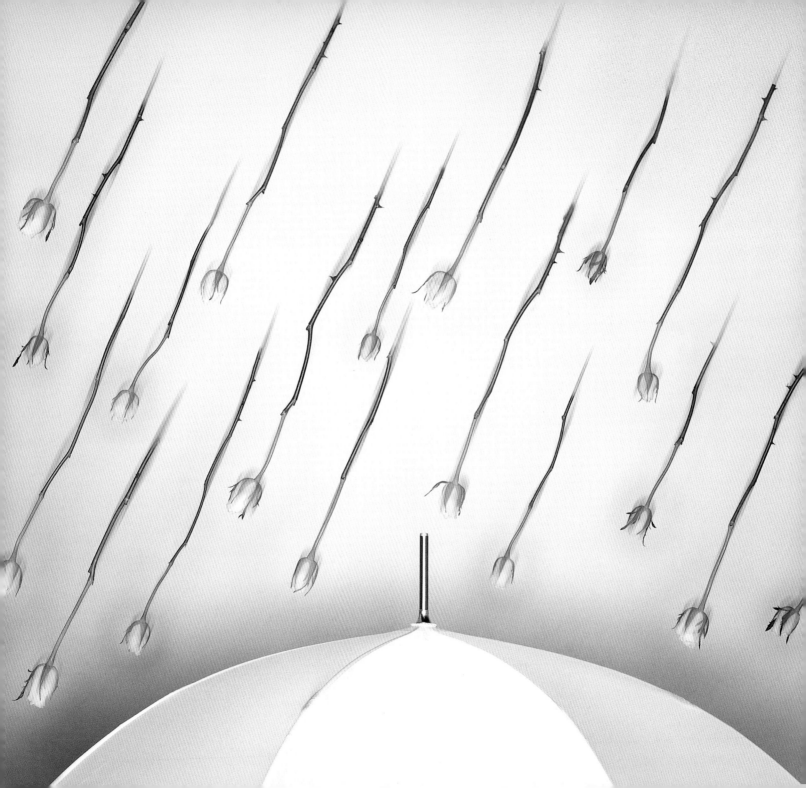

Paying honour with the white rose : THERE IS A TALE OF A

RITUAL FROM TIMES LONG PAST, WHICH I LOVE, AND WHICH DERIVES FROM MY ITALIAN FAMILY. It tells of a family of good people who had fallen on hard times, but in the bleak winter they gathered up all the remaining roses in the garden and laid them out as follows. Their blessings following this ritual were manifold. You might try this to cheer your own heart in the chilly days and see afterward what luck is attracted to you. Indeed. something surprising always seems to happen... **⚬** GO INTO THE GARDEN OR A PARK OR PUBLIC PLACE WHERE YOU CAN FIND A STATUE DEDICATED TO A LADY. Traditionally this was Diana, the lady of the bow, but any female statue will draw pleasure from the sleeping goddess. No matter how poor the weather (best of all if it is snowing), adorn the statue with a little ivy or greenery and a few white roses. If you have no roses you may use hellebores if you have them growing in your garden (though be careful of their toxicity and wash your hands well at the end). Scatter a ring of drops of rose oil or rosewater around the base of the statue and say: *"Lovely goddess of the bow (or lovely lady in marble or metal etc.), you who wake in the starry heavens after the pale sun sinks in the winter sky, with the moon glimmering on your brow; lovely lady, who recalls your sisters sleeping in the earth, and who has known the days of nymphs and music here around you in warmer times; most gracious and most beauteous lady, who knows the powers to endure, think but for an instant on me, and on those of us who are here now who take pleasure in adorning you, and returning your wintry state to a summer haven."* **⚬** YOU SHOULD BOW TO THE LADY AND THEN INVITE A GIRLFRIEND WHO HAS BEEN IN DISTRESS OR HAD A PRESSURED TIME AROUND TO YOUR HOME FOR A DRINK OR SOME FOOD. Show sisterly feeling and invite male friends as well if you like. Give your friend a few white flowers – especially roses – to go home with. When you go to bed yourself, scatter a few white rose petals on your pillow. **⚬** VERY SOON, PERHAPS EVEN BY THE MORNING, A SIGN OF FORTUNE WILL PRESENT ITSELF TO YOU, AND TO YOUR FRIEND.

SPECIAL DATES

We
all have individual days of
significance. They may fall on any
moon, in any month, being anniversaries of
important beginnings or meetings. Sometimes they
are days over which we have little control in terms of
dates, but which will exert a lasting influence. It may be
the date of completion of a house sale, or perhaps a date on
which an exam will fall, or a baby will be induced rather
than born naturally or, even more out of our control, the day
on which we lose a loved one. Whenever these significant
events take place, the dates will be remembered year after
year, and it is important to mark them with our own
special ceremony, and to choose a way of celebrating or,
in the last case, mourning. Here, we look at
traditional ways of marking these individual
dates, providing us with many ideas for
giving them a special, magical
connection.

A ritual for birth : You can't really pick the date on which your baby arrives.

I have heard wondrous tales of mums holding on with sheer determination to give birth on a particular day, but realistically we must accept what nature decrees. So, marking the actual date with appropriate magical signs is a way of heralding a lucky blending between child and the earth and gods. ❦ FIRSTLY, MARK THE ACTUAL DAY OF THE WEEK IN CONNECTION WITH THE BABY. If it were born on a Monday, for instance, ask for a gift of a little moonstone or a pearl and keep it safely, with a particular sense that this little one is in some way especially close to the moon. If it were a Friday, make a symbolic connection between Venus and the child – perhaps buying a tiny rose bush in his or her honour. Check each day (in Chapter 1) for ideas for the appropriate day for you. ❦ ON THE DAY OF THE BIRTH ITSELF, WEAVE MELODY AROUND THE NEWLY ARRIVING BABY SO THAT THE TINY INDIVIDUAL ENTERS INTO A POWERFUL AND LOVING 'SONG-LINE' – this could be a simple unaccompanied song of welcome. It is also a Pagan tradition to take a print – in ink, clay or plaster – of the tiny baby's hand and keep it cherished, decorating it with flowers on important days. ❦ RITUALS FOR THE BIRTH OF A GIRL INCLUDE BURNING ROSE OR ORANGE BLOSSOM INCENSE, AND WEAVING, PAINTING OR MOSAIC-SETTING A SPIRAL IN PINK/MAUVE HUES. She could also be honoured with a newly planted tree, hung with a copper plaque engraved with her name. Choose birch, the silver goddess tree, or rowan, the beautiful but small tree of prosperity that welcomes the new soul. A boy should be welcomed with benzoin, sandal- or cedar-wood incense. Make a wand from hazel or olive wood, carved with his name, and plant a baby oak or ash tree, or an olive or eucalyptus if you're in a warmer country. For a baby of either sex, make a wreath-shaped pillow or cushion inscribed with the date of birth and the names of the child, and stuff the pillow with roses and lavender buds for love and protection. ❦ ADULTS, TOO, CAN HAVE SYMBOLIC 'BIRTH' DAYS – perhaps into a new way of life, or identity, or to a new country, or a new name via marriage or choice. Or perhaps you are giving a newborn baby a naming ceremony rather than a christening. A name-day ritual could incorporate some of the above, and friends should be invited to a little feast. Most importantly, live music of some sort should be played to tell the gods of the arrival of a beautiful new spirit and to ask for their blessings.

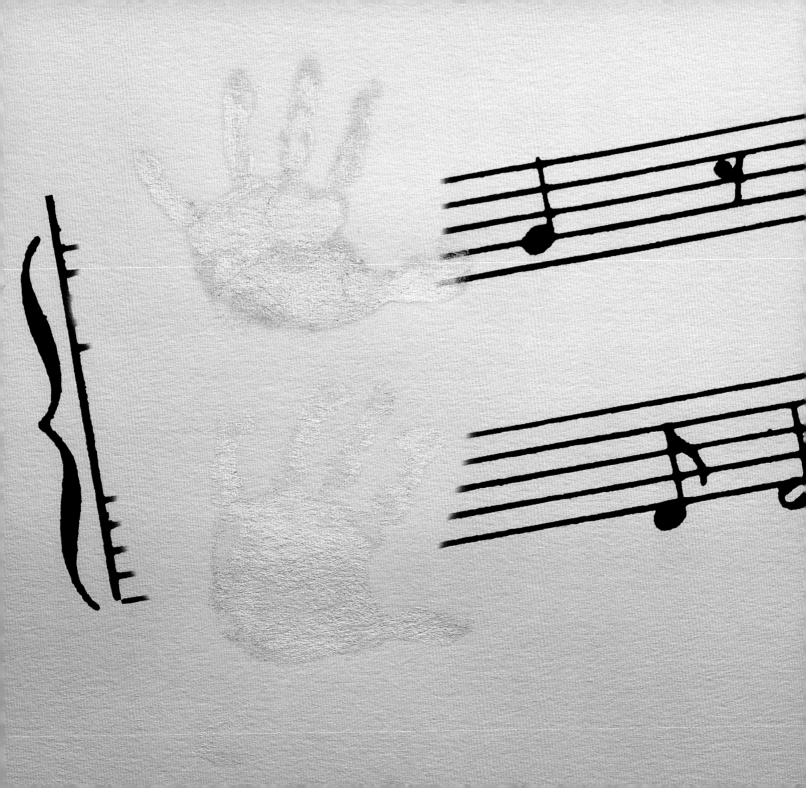

A coming of age ritual : THE TRADITIONAL 21ST BIRTHDAY, COMPLETE WITH THE

MANDATORY KEY, WAS REPLACED BY THE 18TH AS AN ARRIVAL AT ADULTHOOD. But beyond the social occasion of having a great party with plenty of free-flowing refreshment, some of you may prefer to mark the occasion in a more spiritual way, in lieu of the traditional birthday, or in addition. Here are some approaches. ❧ THIS SHOULD BE AN ANNOUNCEMENT TO THE WORLD OF MEN AND GODS THAT A YOUNG PERSON HAS ARRIVED INTO ADULT RESPONSIBILITIES AND DECISIONS. The day should be accompanied by the presentation of an item made from deer-horn or hide, because traditionally a reindeer is seen as the animal of higher spirit, able to survive under any conditions, an altogether free spirit. My husband was given a pair of reindeer boots from Norway, which suit well with his North American heritage – a European equivalent perhaps of beautiful deerskin moccasins. For a smaller item, a reindeer-horn spoon is ideal, and it is not necessary to dress like a morris dancer! There are many beautiful items made from horn and others that may be symbolic of this, such as silver horns. ❧ IN FORMER TIMES, THE ARRIVAL AT ADULTHOOD WAS OFTEN ACCOMPANIED BY THE GIFT OF SALT. A salt cellar made in silver, element of the moon and wisdom, would offer powerful magic to the young initiate, giving him or her unity with the sea and spirit. Salt is still regarded as a lucky magnet for drawing your living and many superstitions and traditions talk of taking salt into a new home to be sure of prosperity.

❧ ON THIS SPECIAL BIRTHDAY OF ADULTHOOD, TAKE A GROUP OF FRIENDS TO A HIGH PLACE AND LIGHT A SMALL FIRE TO MARK THE MOVEMENT ON TO THE NEXT PHASE OF THE WHEEL OF LIFE'S EXPERIENCE. You can do this very discreetly by arranging a picnic on a hill, or even a ferris wheel excursion! A balloon ride would be a wonderful modern evocation of this ritual of high places. Symbolically, you can now see the world from a more objective and higher perspective.

To celebrate a betrothal : RINGS HAVE ALWAYS BEEN EXCHANGED AT ENGAGEMENTS

BECAUSE THEY ARE MADE BY HAND, ARE PRECIOUS AND SYMBOLISE – like a wreath – perpetuation of the love and passion cycle. It is in the spirit of this, something precious and eternal, that a ring is given. ❊ A MAGICAL CONTRIBUTION TO THE TRADITION OF THE RING WOULD BE TO PRESENT IT IN A NATURAL ITEM (SUCH AS A WALNUT SHELL OR CORN HUSK) TO SYMBOLISE TRUTH AND ATTRACT GOOD FORTUNE. The Romans regarded the walnut as the most important emblem of fidelity and luck in marriage because the walnut itself resembles the human brain. For this reason, the wedding cake was made with fruit and nuts, bestowing prosperity, fidelity and fecundity. The corn husk is a more recent tradition, initiated by the Celts who saw the wheat sheaf as a symbol of fertility. ❊ IF YOU PREFER THAT LITTLE BLUE BOX FROM TIFFANY (LUCKY YOU!), YOU MIGHT ADD A SWEET INGREDIENT TO THE WRAPPING OR INSIDE THE LITTLE BOX, SUCH AS COLOURED OR BOILED SUGAR OR SWEETS, TO ATTRACT SWEETNESS AND LUCK AS WELL AS LASTING LOVE. Sugar is a frequent ingredient in magic, as it was so precious and a preservative in life, thus also in love. A very simple ring presented in a little bottle of coloured sugar would draw on the power of sweet thought, association, and beauty; it would also recall the medieval value of sugar as the most prized commodity. ❊ IF YOU WANT TO CAPTURE THE PROPER ENERGY OF WAXING RHYTHM, THE ENGAGEMENT ITSELF SHOULD TAKE PLACE NEAR BELTANE. May is the month for the full expression of fertile intent, and the May 1st sunrise would be a powerful moment to pledge love and propose to your sweetheart.

Wedding days : THE PAGAN FORM OF MARRIAGE IS KNOWN AS HANDFASTING AND SHOULD

IDEALLY TAKE PLACE AS A DUAL EVENT UNFOLDING AROUND MAY 1ST (for the proposal or declaration of feeling, privately and then publicly) and culminating in a high-summer hand-fasting ceremony, traditionally around the Summer Solstice itself. This echoes the perceived marriage of the god and goddess and has long influenced the popularity of a June bride. ❣ THE WITCHES' CEREMONY IS DEDICATED TO A PLEDGE OF LOYALTY BETWEEN THE PAIR WHICH WILL LAST 'A YEAR AND A DAY', THEN TO BE RENEWED IN PUBLIC IN THE FORM OF AN ANNIVERSARY. A year and a day will preserve the original date rather than the day of the week, which is why all our anniversaries move from a Monday to a Tuesday the following year, and so on. The date is more important than the day, so choose it with care; but the original day of the week is also important as it carries the original spirit and luck, setting things in motion. So think about this, too, when you choose your day for the ceremony. Oddly enough Saturday, which is the most popular day because of inviting friends to the ceremony, is probably the least lucky day! Try instead to choose a Friday, which is dedicated to Venus; or a Wednesday, when you have Woden with you, which is powerful indeed.

The handfasting ceremony : THE COUPLES FIRST GRASP THEIR RIGHT

HANDS TOGETHER, PLEDGING THEIR LOGICAL/MASCULINE SOULS TOGETHER; they then slip into a half circle and grasp left hands, creating the artistic/sensitive/female bond between them. Note that both partners contribute both parts of the 'gendered' hemispheres – left and right – the male and female inherent in us all. Both hands may now grip one another and be held crossed, signalling interchange, seeing the world through the loved one's eyes. Then each partner should hold either end of a stick of oak or hazel and wave it thrice through a sacred flame or incense smoke. Petals are strewn to indicate favour on the blessing and to 'naturalise' the relationship. Rose petals are usual, as this is the flower of the goddess of love. ❣ IF YOU DON'T WANT TO PERFORM A FULL HANDFASTING, YOU MIGHT JUST PUT ONE OR TWO ELEMENTS INTO A MORE TRADITIONAL SERVICE. The crossing of both hands, for instance, could be a gentle addition to a civil or other religious service, and petals could be strewn in place of confetti, which is the modern replacement for the flowers themselves. You will understand the significance, even if your friends are none the wiser!

To mark an anniversary : There are so many key moments which become

SIGNIFICANT IN OUR LIVES; each one can be marked individually as a particular anniversary. Originally the passage of one moon (or month) was marked for events like births and relationships and deaths, and these were known as a 'month mind'. The power of the sun brings new energy to the movement of human beings and relationships, so the practice of marking an anniversary annually is more common now. ❧ CELEBRATING ANNIVERSARIES OF RELATIONSHIPS IS RELATIVELY EASY, THE EXCHANGE OF GIFTS AND FLOWERS RECALLING THE CUSTOM OF PERPETUATING PROVIDENCE MAGICALLY BY GIVING SOMETHING TO SOMEONE SPECIAL. Any gift tied with ribbon actually adds magic, for the precious, tactile, colourful properties of ribbons always made them the perfect token of any love. The old song about Johnny away at the fair, which recalls, *"He promised to buy me a bunch of blue ribbons"*, tells us that the hopeful heroine was about to receive a gift pledging his complete loyalty to her. The habit of tying flowers with ribbon is derived from this. Other events require a little more thought. ❧ TO CELEBRATE THE SOLAR RETURN OF AN IMPORTANT DATE SUCH AS THE LAUNCH OF A BUSINESS, or your arrival in a new home, or perhaps even a change of residence from one country to another, draws providence to the event and makes spiritual obeisance to the gods for their favour. It also asks for perpetuation of this providence for another year of good grace.

A silken gift : An anniversary token with magical symbolic significance would be a silk

SQUARE OF HANDKERCHIEF ANOINTED WITH A FEW DROPS OF WATER FROM A SACRED OR SPECIAL PLACE – this could even be the overnight dew from the centre of a beautiful flower. ❧ ON THE ACTUAL DAY WHICH YOU MAY IN FUTURE WISH TO COMMEMORATE, PERFORM THIS RITUAL. First, sprinkle the moisture into the centre of the handkerchief, then a few grains of sea salt and, finally, tie some ribbon around the centre. Choose yellow-gold for a business launch and all its anniversaries, rose-pink or red for emotional connections, green if the celebration concerns a return to health and blue if it has any connection with a home. Then pass the handkerchief through incense and take it to an altar where it must be honoured with a lit candle for one week. After this, place or hang the silken pouch in a quiet place, undisturbed, for a year. With it may go papers connected with the event being commemorated, such as a travel ticket or business card or house key. It may at any time be wrapped in tissue or cellophane and filed away with your important papers. It could also be placed in a picture frame, with petals from a scented flower alongside. Make the whole item as aesthetic as possible.

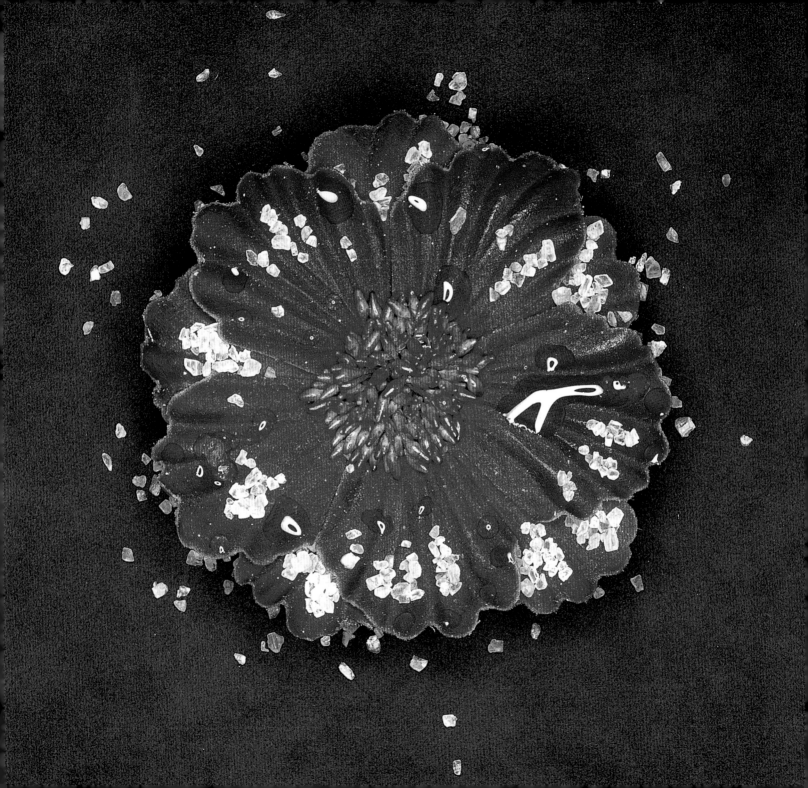

Passing on : OUR LAST SUBJECT IS A TENDER ONE. The most difficult journey is that which takes a loved one from our realm. No matter the comfort gleaned from the individual's possible preparedness and strength, we are stretching the bonds between the knowledge of someone's presence near us and the faith that their spirit is somehow still nearby. There are some poignant gestures that can help to mark the loss and release heartfelt sorrow. ❷ IF SOMEONE IS DYING, AND KNOWS IT, YOU MIGHT SUGGEST THEY REAR AND TEND A FAVOURITE PLANT OR TREE, AND SUGGEST THAT YOU WILL CONTINUE TO TEND THE PLANT TO MAINTAIN THE LIVING BOND BETWEEN YOUR HANDS AND THEIRS. This can be quite a comfort to both parties. The tree could then be planted just after the passing to connect the realms of earth and sky, matter and spirit, and generate growing and ongoing love. ❷ IF YOU ARE PRESENT AS A LOVED ONE PASSES AWAY, SEND BEAUTIFUL GREEN LIGHT AROUND THE FADING LIFE FORCE TO EASE PAIN OR ANXIETY AND PROVIDE TRANQUILLITY. The age-old and universal tradition of lighting a candle illuminates the path for the loved one to find their way through darkness to the new realm. ❷ THERE IS A POIGNANT PAGAN PRACTICE IN WHICH THE BODY WAS PLACED INTO A WOMB-LIKE MOUND TO BLUR THE LINE BETWEEN LIFE AND DEATH, death and rebirth, returning the person to a new pre-birth state in readiness, back into the embrace of the earth mother. It may help you to express your grief if you sit by an ancient tumulus to connect with the inner world of the earth and its mothering spirit. If you have no mound near you, find a space that feels ancient and undisturbed and reflect in your own time, shedding tears of sadness and experiencing emotion as you feel inclined. You might create a small memorial mound in your garden, burying one special object that speaks to you of the soul concerned. Plant up the mound with bulbs and flowers and allow it to go grassy only in the winter, symbolically re-enacting life and rebirth. ❷ IF YOU HAVE NOT HAD A CHANCE TO SAY 'GOODBYE' TO THE DEPARTED SOUL, WRITE THEM A LETTER FROM THE HEART, THEN BURY IT WITH THE LOVED ONE; it is a private treaty of understanding between you and them alone. In one of my favourite Pagan rituals an acorn was buried with the body (or in the ashes) so the spirit of the soul could blossom forth thereafter in a mighty tree. ❷ SEND THE INDIVIDUAL OFF WITH A HUGE UPSURGE OF LOVE: try not to lament and hold back their progress to the earth, but sing them on their astral way, part of the everlasting energy source of light and mystery. A ring of votive candles in glass holders at the graveside or around a tree would be a special way of lighting the path ahead both for you and the one you have lost.

Index